BREAK INTO FICTION®

11 STEPS TO BUILDING A STORY THAT SELLS

MARY BUCKHAM AND DIANNA LOVE

Adamsmedia
Avon, Massachusetts

Published by
Adams Media, a division of F+W Media, Inc.
57 Littlefield Street, Avon, MA 02322. U.S.A.
www.adamsmedia.com

ISBN 10: 1-60550-015-1
ISBN 13: 978-1-60550-015-7

Printed in the United States of America.

J I H G F E D C B A

Library of Congress Cataloging-in-Publication Data
is available from the publisher.

This publication is designed to provide accurate and authoritative information with regard to the subject matter covered. It is sold with the understanding that the publisher is not engaged in rendering legal, accounting, or other professional advice. If legal advice or other expert assistance is required, the services of a competent professional person should be sought.

—From a *Declaration of Principles* jointly adopted by a Committee of the American Bar Association and a Committee of Publishers and Associations

Many of the designations used by manufacturers and sellers to distinguish their product are claimed as trademarks. Where those designations appear in this book and Adams Media was aware of a trademark claim, the designations have been printed with initial capital letters.

This book is available at quantity discounts for bulk purchases.
For information, please call 1-800-289-0963.

To writers striving to be published . . .
we wrote this book for you.

Contents

Part III. Don't Let Them Put the Book Down 195

Acknowledgments

We'd like to thank all the unpublished writers and published authors who have shared their time and insights with us. Your thirst for knowledge and sincere desire to push your story to another level encouraged us to build this program into what it is today. An extra thank-you to all the students we've met while presenting workshops.

Every good book has a wonderful editor behind it and this one is no different. It has been a pleasure working with Paula Munier of Adams Media. Her enthusiasm for this project has made all the difference. We also want to thank our agent, Merrilee Heifetz, who is extraordinary in every way.

Many years ago, writers had few places to go for help, but today there is an amazing support base of writing organizations across the country. We'd like to thank the endless number of writing organizations who have invited us to their cities to speak on this program.

There would be no book without both of our husbands—Jim (Mary's) and Karl (Dianna's)—they are exceptional men who understand that living with writers means the word *normal* goes right out the window.

A special thank-you to #1 *New York Times* best-selling author Sherrilyn Kenyon; she supported this project from day one, allowed us to use text from one of her novels, and even agreed to pen the foreword to our book.

If not for the authors who came before us, we would have had no one to learn from. Two more of the wonderful authors whose work we learned from also gave us permission to use some of their work for examples in this book: *New York Times* best-selling author Suzanne

Brockmann and legal thriller author Ed Gaffney. Thank you and all the others for helping writers everywhere!

Mary: Writing any book—fiction or nonfiction—is hard work. Writing with a cowriter like Dianna made the hard work fun and worth every moment. Dianna can balance writing a *New York Times* bestselling book in between giving Break Into Fiction® workshops, writing this book, and having a life. Here's a huge thank-you to her, to her husband Karl for great meals, and to Jim, my husband, for being there always.

Dianna: I would like to thank my cowriter and Break Into Fiction® partner, Mary Buckham, who was the original template queen. Mary is an exceptional mystery-suspense author, an outstanding instructor, and a great business partner. It's been a pleasure working on this book with her and I'm looking forward to doing many more. And, a special thanks to Karl, my husband—without him there would be no books at all. I'd go on for pages, but we'd never get to the important part— plotting *your* book!

Foreword

by #1 *New York Times* best-selling author Sherrilyn Kenyon

Crafting a novel can be one of the most rewarding accomplishments for any person . . . and one of the most frustrating.

I'm a pantser, which means I write a book by the seat of my pants. Or more specifically, I sit down to a blank sheet of paper and start typing. So you may wonder why I'm writing the foreword to a book on power plotting. The answer is simple: This book isn't about converting pantsers to plotting, but about helping anyone who needs help with their story.

I started creating stories as soon as I could write. Some people have the natural ability to sit down and type without any plan. I always knew I wanted to write books, so I'm thankful for being born with this gift. But on top of that, I also have years of experience that have taught me how to develop characters, build in conflict, and catch plot holes. You can do the same if you're content with taking as many years as you need to learn the craft of writing. If not, this book will help for a faster learning curve.

What I love about what Mary and Dianna teach is that their intent is not to convert pantsers to be plotters, but to give both types of writers tools for breaking through writer's block or finding a plot hole or shoring up a sagging middle. I have to assume you picked up this book because you want to write your first novel or find a way to push your current one to a new level or are published and seeking a more efficient way to plot a book.

Writers ask me, "How do you write a publishable novel for today's market?" I wish I could answer that in one sentence or had the time to teach everyone, but I don't. The good news is that Mary and Dianna created the Break Into Fiction® program to answer that question. They pulled together the essential elements of commercial fiction into an easy-to-understand book that anyone can follow.

You're holding the key to plotting your novel. The most important tip I can give you next is to finish the book. Good luck to you no matter where you are in your career. Remember, good books aren't written, they're rewritten. Just because it's written in blood doesn't mean that it's carved in stone.

And most importantly, never give up. Never surrender. I wish you all success and may all the publishing gods be with you.

Introduction

This *is* the book you need to create a novel. Why? Because we have spent many years and thousands of hours analyzing commercial fiction for one purpose: to discover what it takes to turn a story idea into a marketable novel. The result of all this work was the creation of Break Into Fiction®, a Template Teaching Series that simplifies the process of how to build a full story with realistic characters.

As national workshop speakers, we have gained valuable insights into how today's new writers want to learn the craft of writing. We interact with thousands of aspiring writers every year who want to know what it will take to publish in today's market. Having broken into the ranks of published fiction authors only a few years ago, we understand what the next generation of new writers must do to produce a marketable novel. Until now, writers were faced with first attending hours of workshops and reading tomes, then struggling to remember all the many facets of information when they finally had a chance to use that information in their writing.

Frustrated with this antiquated method, we have created innovative templates for plotting a novel.

The response to this style of teaching, Character-Driven Plotting, was overwhelmingly positive.

If you're ready to write a novel, then this is your book. You don't need a cheerleader. You've already made the mental decision to write, because you're holding the book that will put you on that path. You're ready to get started. However, wanting to write a book and doing it are two different things. A first-year med student doesn't ask when they get to perform brain surgery—they know there's a logical progression of steps to get there. At some point they are ready to step forward to reach their dream. The learning separates those who *want* to do something and those who *do* it. Put one foot in front of another and get moving.

Great stories don't happen by accident. They are the result of creating a powerful Character-Driven Plot. Writing a novel can seem like a daunting task, but it is no different than anything else you've had to learn . . . once it's broken down into simple steps. There is no formula for writing a book. But the instructions and templates in this book are akin to handing a fine brush to an artist, and then showing a student how to apply paint to his or her own canvas. The final product is different for everyone depending on how gently the brush is wielded and how boldly the paint is applied. You have an idea for a story—that's why you're holding this book. Now, turn the page so we can show you how professional writers develop a budding idea into a full-fledged novel with depth, emotion, and dynamic pacing. Start right from the first chapter on *your* story. We commend you for taking this first step toward your dream.

How to Use This Book

Break Into Fiction® Movie Template Instruction

We want you to start writing your book immediately. The quickest way to take advantage of this material and start writing your commercial fiction story is by watching the movies we use for examples. These four movies were chosen to show you how successful commercial fiction has key elements. This process makes understanding the instruction and templates so simple you're ready to apply what you learn to your story immediately. If you're a fairly new writer, choose one movie and go through all the templates with that one story so that you aren't confused by too much information at one time. Once you've done that, watch the other movies and see how these templates work with every story.

Bourne Identity (2002—Universal Pictures)—Suspense

Jason Bourne (Matt Damon) as the protagonist

Marie (Franka Potente) as a major secondary character

Conklin (Chris Cooper) as the villain (CIA handler)

Ward Abbott (Brian Cox) as the villain (Conklin's boss at CIA)

Pretty Woman (1990—Touchstone Pictures)—Romantic Comedy

Edward Lewis (Richard Gere) as the hero

Vivian Ward (Julia Roberts) as the heroine

Phillip Stuckey (Jason Alexander) as the antagonist/villain

James Morse (Ralph Bellamy) as the mentor/business owner

Casablanca (1942—Warner Pictures)

Rick Blaine (Humphrey Bogart) as the protagonist

Ilsa Lund (Ingrid Bergman) as the antagonist/love interest

Victor Laszlo (Paul Henreid) as the antagonist

Captain Renault (Claude Rains) as the antagonist

Finding Nemo (2003—Walt Disney Pictures)

Marlin (voice of Albert Brooks) as the protagonist

Dory (voice of Ellen DeGeneres) as the mentor/ally

The Glossary is next for an important reason. Read through the Glossary, since you'll be encountering terminology specific to the Break Into Fiction® Character-Driven Plotting Program. Becoming familiar with these terms will help you grasp examples more quickly. If you want to make a copy of the blank templates to work from, you can enlarge the book page 160 percent for a letter-sized sheet. Another way is to write the chapter heading and question numbers on a sheet of paper in a notebook, then fill in the answers.

Glossary

Ally—Someone who helps the protagonist or another character as they strive to achieve a specific set of actions. This role can be a temporary story function for the character—as in one scene—or an ongoing story function such as Dory's story role in *Finding Nemo*.

Antagonist—[Might or might not be the villain, and can be another character in a story with a villain.] This is a character who opposes the protagonist, but is not always a bad person. In many stories, the antagonist is actually working in what the antagonist considers the protagonist's best interest (think a business partner who believes his buddy is falling for the wrong woman or a teacher who won't quit on a student who has potential). In a romance, the antagonist is usually the hero to the heroine or heroine to the hero.

Back Story—Information on a character that gives the reader insights and motivation for why this particular character acts or reacts as they do, based on a past event or events. Back story is meant to be filtered into your story in small doses or used as twists to the plot line.

Belief System—Usually subconscious to a character, the belief system drives the actions of a character to act in a certain way unless the belief system changes. Most belief systems are established in childhood by watching and learning from others or in times of extreme emotion. Belief systems can usually be identified by asking the question, "*If* X, *then* Y." Examples: "*If* you take a risk, *then* you can get burned badly," or "*If* you love enough, *then* everything can be fixed." A belief system can be either positive or negative, and it helps form a character's world view.

Black Moment—A term used in the romance genre to identify the story Climax. See *Climax*, which is the terminology used in our plotting templates.

Character's Everyday World Role—This is what the character has been *typecast* for in the story—hooker, attorney, temporary girlfriend, past lover, famous freedom fighter, etc. The role merely tags who this character is with regard to actual scenes.

Character's External Story Goal—(This may or may not be the same as the Character's Immediate External Goal.) This is a goal you (the writer) plan and target for the character to reach at the end of the story. A Character's Immediate External Goal (the one the character knows about and is going after) in the beginning may be the same as the External Story Goal for this character (the one you, the writer, intend the character to reach and/or accomplish) in the end. However, due to situations that impact the character's journey, this goal may morph into a new one.

Character's Immediate External Goal—(This may or may not be the same as the External Story Goal.) This is an external goal the character has in sight at the beginning and at different points along the way in the story. These are immediate goals (to find the murderer, save a job, find the source of a virus, pay the rent, etc.) that the character is motivated to perform or pursue that lead the character to a larger external story goal.

Character's Story Role—This is a technical story term for either the protagonist or a secondary character, broken down further by type—such as a mentor, antagonist, sidekick, rival, tempter—which clarifies this character's job description.

Climax—This is the third twist point in commercial fiction where the protagonist must face a death of sorts (physical, metaphorical, emotional) in order to make one last extra effort to reach the Character's External Story Goal. The act of facing and overcoming the obstacle stopping him/her/it at this point will forever change the character and creates the reassurance in a reader's mind that the story lessons that have been learned along the way in the story will be retained after the last page is turned. Example: In *Finding Nemo*, Marlin's story climax happens when his friend, Dory, and hundreds of other fish are nabbed by a trawler's nets. At this point, Marlin could swim away and return home or make a super-fish effort to free Dory, showing that the lessons he's learned (about taking risks, finding friends, and acting in the face of threats instead of cowering) are permanent. In romance fiction, the climax is also known as a "Black Moment."

Commercial Fiction—Fiction with a specific structure that includes a protagonist or protagonists striving toward a goal with obstacles encountered and overcome until they reach a do-or-die moment (Climax) where they must make one huge last effort to prevail or fail. The story ends on a positive note of some sort. Due to the events encountered over the course of the story, the protagonist experiences Internal Character Growth and changes as a result. Commercial fiction derives from myths and fairy tales, and is often called "genre fiction." It is based on the reader's belief system that if they try hard enough they can achieve something and make a change in their world for the better. Romances, mysteries, suspense, thrillers, science fiction (often called "sci-fi"), fantasy, etc., are commercial fiction genres.

Conflict—This is what drives the story forward and creates pacing. Conflict is not an argument or issue that can be resolved with a conversation. Think: two hungry dogs, one bone.

Everyday World—This is what the protagonist considers their normal world at the beginning of a story. Don't confuse this with where they grew up or how they lived a year ago. In other words, if the story starts when a young man is in college, his Everyday World is how he lives and interacts while in college. However, if the story begins after this same man has joined the military and he is now part of a Special Forces team, his Everyday World at that point might open in a Special Ops mission.

Foreshadowing—This is a technique that uses hints and clues to let a reader know in advance that something in the story is about to change. Foreshadowing also lays the groundwork for establishing events later in your story. Example: In Chapter 2 of your story, you foreshadow that the character has a deathly fear of heights. Then when the character is forced to wrestle the villain atop a twenty-story building in Chapter 10, a reader is aware that this event is not an easy undertaking,

Happily Ever After (HEA)—A term used most often by romance writers, but it can apply to any commercial fiction. HEA means that the reader feels the protagonist(s) will find a better future beyond the end of the story, and the hero and heroine will end up together.

Herald—This character role explains the rules of the situation, particularly if it is a new situation for the protagonist. This character role can also be used to announce events and establish proper behavior expectations.

Inciting Incident—A catalyst that puts the story into motion.

Internal Character Growth—This is a *Break Into Fiction*® term that best explains what will happen internally for the protagonist over the course of the story. These are stages of internal growth *you* (the writer) plan for the character. The complete growth arc starts with where the character is internally at the beginning of the story, includes the stages of personal development along the way, and is completed when the character reaches the final stage of their Internal Character Growth. Most people have no idea what their personal journey is in life until they've traveled that path, so you, as the writer, are in charge of your character's ability to grow as a human being. This has nothing to do with personal career success or reaching a dream of becoming the top ice skater in the world, but the internal changes that happen along the way to those "external" goals.

Literary Fiction—Not to be confused with literature, Literary Fiction is based on the reader's belief system that one cannot change their world but they can understand it better. The plot structure of literary fiction does not move toward a specific goal but involves peeling away the emotions and dark secrets of the human condition in an attempt to understand better. The protagonist in literary fiction need not grow or change over the course of the story.

Mentor—This is a character who gives your main character advice and direction (think Dory in *Finding Nemo* to the main character Marlin), and may be the one to give the main character his or her Seeds of Change. This is an advisory character role, which will help or force the protagonist to take action that he or she may not otherwise want to take. The Mentor allows the reader to see that even though action is difficult for the primary character, they are given strong enough motivation to act anyway. Note: A mentor is a "catalyst" as well as a guide or advisor, and at times there may be more than one mentor in your story.

Motivation—This is what drives your character's actions, the reason your character must make a decision or take an action. Tip: Motivation is *not* making the character do something or act a certain way because the author "needs" that to happen. Poor motivation stops the reader from moving forward.

Pacing—This is the speed at which events in the story unfold. Different sections of the book require different pacing speeds and different genres can have very different pacing expectations. A suspense or thriller story should be paced from fast to very fast, whereas women's fiction or a "cozy" mystery can have a slower-paced tempo.

POV—This is an acronym for Point of View, which refers to the character through whose eyes, thoughts, and senses we are experiencing the current scene. A first-person POV means the story is being told and experienced through one person's point of view as if that person were speaking directly to you; such as, "I drove along the winding highway, searching for the street sign that would lead me to the killer's hideout."

The same sentence in third-person POV would be, "Mary drove along the winding highway, searching for the street sign that would lead her to the killer's hideout." Omniscient POV is a third-person narrator who is telling how Mary is driving along the winding highway and as she turns off the main highway, she is heading straight to her death.

Premise Stated—Often used in conjunction with the word *theme;* both mean something that's been laid out in advance by the author that determines a future course for the protagonist. It's the underlying meaning and essence of your story that many times can be reduced to a key word or phrase. Think in terms of a single idea, ideal, or quality such as love, betrayal, revenge, family, or connection; or a phrase such as "truth wins out," "no man is an island," or "an honest man always triumphs."

Prologue—The prologue should be an inciting incident that occurs a significant amount of time before you shift to the protagonist's Every-day World in the first chapter. The prologue is considered your story opening and should not be used as an information dump to get your character's Back Story stated.

Protagonist—This is the character who will experience the most Internal Character Growth and change over the course of the story.

Sagging Middle—A common term used to describe the middle of a novel where if not tightly woven and plotted with twist points can slow pacing and serve no strong story function. The most common result of a Sagging Middle is for readers to lose interest in the story and put the book down.

Secondary Story Line—(This story line should not to be confused with Subplot.) This is a secondary story that adds texture to the main plot, but the main plot would still hold together if this secondary story line was removed. Here is an example: In *Finding Nemo*, the secondary story line is Nemo interacting with the other fish in the dentist office aquarium. This interaction adds texture to the story, because we get to see Nemo find another adult father-figure who gives Nemo different information and insights. But the story is about Marlin's (Nemo's father) Internal Character Growth (internal growth arc) while searching for his son. If you removed the secondary story from the dentist office aquarium the main plot would still hold up.

Seeds of Change—The section of your story where the protagonist is poised to make a change, whether voluntary or involuntary. Because the protagonist is willing to try to change for the betterment of themselves or others, they start their story arc. If the story remains static and no change is made, the story becomes Literary Fiction.

Series—Stories linked by a common protagonist, protagonists, or story thread. In Sherrilyn Kenyon's Dark-Hunter stories, the books are linked by a common thread of powerful nonhumans created to protect the world from vampires and other paranormal threats. In J. K. Rowling's Harry Potter stories and in many mystery series, the stories are linked by a common protagonist. The plot structure of each story in a series is impacted by the story or stories that precede it, and in turn will impact any stories that follow.

Subplot—(This should not be confused with a Secondary Story Line.) This is a second plot that is working concurrently with the main plot and is woven so tightly with the main plot the story will fall apart without this Subplot. Example: In *Casablanca*, the subplot is Rick and Ilsa's romantic relationship that drives action in the main plot. Note: *Casablanca* is *not* a romance, but a drama or mainstream suspense with romantic elements. A romance has a clear hero and heroine who are both protagonists, a complete romantic arc, and the hero and heroine end up together in a committed relationship.

Threshold Guardian—This is a person who throws obstacles into the path of the main character as he or she tries to reach their goal. A threshold guardian is usually most effective just before or after a major twist point.

Ticking Clock—A ticking clock is an internal or external element in the story that creates a limit to how long the character has to complete their external goal. This adds tension, which helps the pacing in your story.

Twist Points—These are the key areas of your story where your protagonist is given good, realistic reasons not to continue on his or her current path. But he or she chooses to continue and, as a result, the protagonist is changed and becomes closer to his or her External Story Goal (that you, as the author, know). Each twist point should increase the stakes in the story and make it more difficult for the protagonist to revert to the person he or she was in the beginning of the story. There are three main twist points in the commercial fiction plot structure. The last one is called the "Climax" (or the "Black Moment" in a romance).

Villain—Most of the time, the villain is a character on the same level as the protagonist. The villain is fighting the protagonist for a common goal with the villain's goal to be the final victor.

World View—This is based on a character's Belief System, which influences how that character views the world around them. For example, according to Marlin's (Nemo's father in the movie *Finding Nemo*) Belief System, if he moves beyond the protective shelter of his anemone home, then he and Nemo will be at risk. As a result of this Belief System, Marlin finds the world a large and frightening place.

Part I
START AT THE BEGINNING

Characters
Conflict
Power Openings

Every writer starts from a different place. Inspiration for a story may be a character, a setting, a situation . . . there are as many reasons behind every story as there are stories.

We start with Characters since every commercial fiction story has a protagonist at the center of everything.

Second, the conflict this character faces is what holds our interest. We want to know how another human being will overcome obstacles to succeed. This is the heart of a commercial fiction story, which is why we will dig deep into your character to establish a conflict strong enough to carry your story.

The question is: Where do you open a story? Turn the page to help you answer that.

1

According to Webster's Dictionary, **character** is defined as "A person in a play or novel; distinctive trait; behavior typical of a person or group; moral strength; reputation; status; individual being."

1 CHARACTERS
Created from the Soul Out

"Few men are of one plain, decided color; most are mixed, shaded, and blended; and vary as much, from different situations, as changeable silks do from different lights."

—Lord Chesterfield

There is so much more to creating a real character than choosing physical attributes and personality traits. The most memorable characters stay with us because they touched our emotions and became real people in our minds.

When molding your character, don't stop at the stereotypical basics—she couldn't trust men again, he was trying to win his father's approval, she wanted to prove her independence, he was a loose cannon—if you want him or her to spring off the page.

Build a prior life for your character—to use as reference material for you as a writer, not to fill the pages of your story.

Ed Gaffney writes a legal thriller series based on two law partners—Terry Tallach and Zack Wilson—who are as different as two men can be and share a profession.

Here's an example of how Zack appears from Terry's POV taken from *Suffering Fools*. Notice how deftly the author shares insights about Terry's personality while the focus is really on Zack.

In this scene, Terry isn't happy about the pro bono case Zack has taken for a client who appears mentally challenged and guilty as sin. They are currently interviewing the client's mother. (This scene is in Terry's POV.)

> The victim had ID'd him. What else was there?
>
> Terry turned toward Zack. He sure didn't look like one of the best criminal defense lawyers in the state. As usual, Zack was sporting his I-look-like-I'm-on-vacation look. Linen shirt—sleeves rolled up, of course, probably just to piss Terry off—jeans, and boots.
>
> But despite his stubborn refusal to look the part, Zack always seemed to be surrounded by this golden aura of professionalism. He walked into a courtroom, smiled like he couldn't believe how lucky he was just to be alive, and juries instantly fell in love with him. It was like some genetic accident had left him with an overabundance of charm.
>
> Unfortunately, Zack also had an overabundance of patience.

Don't you love how even though this is in Terry's POV we immediately see "Terry" as impatient and someone who takes exception to casual clothes worn during working hours? We got a nice introduction to Zack without learning every detail about him in one chapter, and in an active way. Now let's take a look at Terry a bit later after the above scene where the defendant's mother, Katerina Gardiner, has handed the two attorneys a videotape she claims is an exact copy of the damning one the police took from the surveillance cameras at the convenience store. But she claims this tape will clear her son of the charges. (This scene is in Zack's POV.)

> *Long after a story ends, it's the characters that remain with you. A great character is one you expect to see in real life just around the next corner.*
>
> —Pat White,
> award-winning author of
> *Ring Around My Heart*

> Attorney Zack Wilson led his partner, Terry Tallach, into the living room, where they planned to view the videotape that Katerina Gardiner swore would prove her son innocent.
>
> "I'm really looking forward to seeing this," Terry told Zack as he sat on the couch. "Because as everyone knows, grand juries indict people all the

time for armed robbery when the police have videotapes that show they are innocent."

Terry's attitude wasn't exactly a surprise. Ever since they'd met, back in high school, the question for Terry wasn't whether the glass was half empty. It was whether what was inside the glass would kill him or just make him sick.

Now, twenty years later, they were successful law partners, and Terry still looked at the world through doom-colored glasses.

You can feel the difference in personalities by the sentence structure and word choice as much as by the descriptions given in a vivid way. You can feel the tenseness in Terry and the calm Zack exudes. Terry is cranky about the tape and Zack is patiently waiting to see what is on it.

Notice how you learn just a little more about their history each time, just enough to start seeing these men as real people, but not so much the story stops moving forward. This is a great way to show a character—through the eyes of another character.

Every piece of the story works together to pull a reader deeper into the character's problems and conflict. The more a reader engages with a character the more interested the reader will be in watching how a character reacts during something as simple as an interview where one character is methodically taking his time and the other one is a mass of energy waiting to be unleashed. We connect to these two men on a personal level as the story unfolds because Ed has created characters that breathe and think on every page.

The key to showing us emotion within a character is to climb inside that person to understand how he or she will react in a given situation. Every personality trait has a positive side and a negative side, depending on your perspective. Take a look at these examples and build a list showing the strengths and weaknesses of major characters in your story.

CHARACTER TRAIT	STRENGTH	WEAKNESS
easygoing	hard to ruffle	slow to act
silent, quiet	thoughtful	emotionally distant
impatient	decisive	acts on impulse
disciplined	dependable	unyielding
sweet	easy to know	a doormat

POWERFUL CHARACTERS TEMPLATE

The purpose of this template is to develop your main character(s) from the inside out (determine what they are lacking internally to be a more complete human being and what their core beliefs are) and to learn what drives this character (motivation) to action. A three-dimensional character strengthens your story and is the central, most important piece of a strong plot. Use the template for your protagonist (note that there are two protagonists in a romance), antagonist(s), and villain(s). Since they should be your strongest characters, allocate the most page space to them.

The Character for this template is:

----

1. What two or three adjectives best define this character?

    TIP: Not externally but internally.

    ----

2. What does this character believe about his or her Everyday World (i.e., that it is a safe place, that they are an outsider, that risk is dangerous, etc.)?

    ----

3. Is the character content with his or her Everyday World at the opening of the story? Why or why not?

    ----

4. What would this character say is his or her strength?

    ----

5. What would this character say is his or her weakness?

    ----

6. What do other story characters see as this character's strength?

    TIP: Describe from several other characters' viewpoints.

    ----

7. What do other story characters see as this character's weakness?

    ----

8. If this character's occupation influences the story in a significant way,
    what is his or her occupation, and how does he or she feel about it?

    ----

9. How are you going to create (show) reader sympathy for this character in
    the opening of your story?

    ----

10. What is lacking internally for this character, even if he or she is not aware of it?

> **TIP:** This is tied directly to the Internal Character Growth you (the author) are planning by the end of the story for this character.

----

11. What does this character value most in life and why?

> **TIP:** This should play a role in motivation for this character's actions.

----

12. What do you, as the author, want as the overall External Story Goal for this character?

> **TIP:** Sometimes the character knows what the ultimate goal is—find a killer, save the planet, reclaim the homestead—but sometimes the character is not willing to face this ultimate goal until actions over the course of the story prepare them to handle the effort needed to reach this final goal. This character will attempt smaller external goals first, such as find a clue, look for a missing person, agree to work closely with a potential love interest. Sometimes the character is very much aware that their one external goal over the course of the story does not change—find the bad guy, stop a bomb, save a historic building. You, as the author, should know the character's overall External Story Goal, even if the character is clearly not aware of what their ultimate external goal is or how difficult it will be to reach.

----

13. What will happen if this character does not reach his or her overall External Story Goal that you, as the author, know must be attempted?

> **TIP:** Think worst case that can happen.

----

14. What does this character want externally at the beginning of the story (his or her most Immediate External Goal)?

> **TIP:** This character may think that one small step is all he or she needs to accomplish, but you know it is a step toward the character's larger External Story Goal.

----

15. What will happen if this character does not reach his or her Immediate External Goal? (There should be something at stake that creates an urgency for this character to reach or accomplish this first external goal, which will translate into motivation.)

----

16. Who does this character trust at the beginning of the story and why?

----

17. Who does this character not trust and why?

----

18. Who will this character trust at the end of the story and why?

---

19. Give an example of how this character will change or grow internally by the end of the story.

> **TIP:** This is the Internal Character Growth you as the author have planned for the character.

---

20. What will be different externally for this character at the end of the story and why?

The Bourne Identity

THE CHARACTER FOR THIS TEMPLATE IS:
Jason Bourne (Matt Damon)

1. What two or three adjectives best define this character?
   Driven, determined, private.

2. What does this character believe about his or her Everyday World?
   Jason believes his Everyday World is a dangerous place for him personally.

3. Is the character content with his or her Everyday World at the opening of the story? Why or why not?
   Jason is not content with his world because he's been shot, he has amnesia, and he fears his past contains dark secrets.

4. What would this character say is his or her strength?
   Being decisive because that's the difference between life and death on the run.

5. What would this character say is his or her weakness?
   Jason's weakness is his amnesia that prevents him from knowing the truth about who he is and what he's done.

6. What do other story characters see as this character's strength?
   Marie sees Jason as dangerous, but sees his skills as a strength that protects them; Jason's immediate CIA boss sees his training as Jason's strength.

7. What do other story characters see as this character's weakness?
   Marie observes Jason's inability to see the good in himself as a weakness; Jason's immediate CIA boss sees Jason's inability to terminate a target regardless of collateral damage to innocents as a weakness.

8. **If this character's occupation influences the story in a significant way, what is his or her occupation, and how does he or she feel about it?**

Jason doesn't know his occupation, but comes to suspect he was some sort of trained killer. The fact that he was a deadly operative with the CIA is a key factor in Jason's motivation to find the truth about himself.

9. **How are you going to create (show) reader sympathy for this character in the opening of your story?**

Waking up with no memory and bullets in his back is something anyone could understand. Additionally, even though Jason has access to guns many times in the story he chooses to leave them behind. That shows that although he knows how to use a gun, his true nature is not to kill people.

10. **What is lacking internally for this character, even if he or she is not aware of it?**

Because of his CIA training, Jason lacks the ability to trust or to connect with other people.

11. **What does this character value most in life and why?**

Jason values his freedom and the truth; he hopes he will be able to attain both through the return of his memory.

12. **What do you, as the author, want as the overall External Story Goal for this character?**

Jason will have to face the CIA individuals who trained him and stop their actions or die trying to stop them.

13. **What will happen if this character does not reach his or her overall External Story Goal that you, as the author, know must be attempted?**

Jason will either be killed by the CIA or he will be on the run for the rest of his life.

14. **What does this character want externally at the beginning of the story (his or her most Immediate External Goal)?**

Jason's most Immediate External Goal is to find out if the Swiss bank vault number found on the capsule in his hip has a clue to his identity.

15. **What will happen if this character does not reach his or her immediate External Goal?**

The Swiss bank vault is Jason's only current option for learning his true identity and someone obviously wants him dead because he woke up with two bullets in his back. Therefore, not reaching that vault and not gaining his identity is life-and-death important because he has no idea who is a threat or who is a friend.

16. **Who does this character trust at the beginning of the story and why?**

At the beginning of the story, Jason gives limited trust to the fishermen who saved him and treated his wounds, because he's forced to accept their help.

17. **Who does this character not trust and why?**

Jason trusts no one because he has no idea who he is and he has no idea who shot him. He also realizes that he's been trained not to trust anyone, although he doesn't know why.

18. **Who will this character trust without question at the end of the story and why?**

Jason will trust Marie without question, because she stayed with him when she could have walked away in spite of knowing he's been trained to be an assassin.

19. **Give an example of how this character will change or grow internally by the end of the story.**

Jason will change from a man on the run who fears he may have been a cold-blooded killer to a man on the attack who is ready to stop the men who send out assassins to kill regardless of the cost.

20. **What will be different externally for this character at the end of the story and why?**

By the end of the story, Jason appears to no longer be on the run from threats and he's connected with Marie.

TIP: There are two protagonists in a romance—the hero and heroine—so fill out a template for each one.

1. **What two or three adjectives best define this character?**

   Loyal, gutsy, and a survivor.

2. **What does this character believe about his or her Everyday World?**

   Vivian believes her Everyday World is a dangerous place to live, but that she doesn't deserve a better life. This world is as good as it'll get for a girl like her.

3. **Is the character content with his or her Everyday World at the opening of the story? Why or why not?**

   Vivian is not content with her Everyday World, because she never planned to be a hooker and she wants security without having to trade her body for it.

4. **What would this character say is his or her strength?**

   Vivian would say her strengths are her personality and her determination.

5. **What would this character say is his or her weakness?**

   Bad judgment of men; being emotionally gullible.

6. **What do other story characters see as this character's strength?**

   Edward sees Vivian's strength as her ability to adapt to any situation and connect emotionally with people.

7. **What do other story characters see as this character's weakness?**

   Vivian's roommate sees Vivian's weakness as making emotional attachments.

8. **If this character's occupation influences the story in a significant way, what is his or her occupation, and how does he or she feel about it?**

   Vivian is a prostitute and does not like it, but feels it's the most she can expect.

9. **How are you going to create (show) reader sympathy for this character in the opening of your story?**

   Even though it means Vivian has to pin her boots together, scrounge food from the bar condiment tray, and must climb out the fire escape to hide from the landlord, she is still willing to help her roommate make up the money her roommate squandered, because her roommate was the only person who helped Vivian when she was desperate.

10. **What is lacking internally for this character, even if he or she is not aware of it?**

    Vivian lacks the ability to believe she deserves a better life than a hooker.

11. **What does this character value most in life and why?**

    Vivian values financial security most in life, because it translates into her own personal safety.

12. **What do you, as the author, want as the overall External Story Goal for this character?**

    That Vivian will find security without trading her body for money, plus leave prostitution for a new future.

13. **What will happen if this character does not reach his or her overall External Story Goal that you, as the author, know must be attempted?**

    Vivian will return to the precarious life of a hooker, living hand-to-mouth and at risk every day.

14. **What does this character want externally at the beginning of the story (his or her most Immediate External Goal)?**

    Vivian wants to make enough money to pay the rent and the drug dealer threatening her roommate.

15. **What will happen if this character does not reach his or her Immediate External Goal?**

    If Vivian fails to find replacement rent money, she and her roommate will be homeless and at the mercy of a dangerous drug dealer wanting to pimp them.

16. **Who does this character trust at the beginning of the story and why?**

    In the beginning, Vivian only trusts her roommate because she helped Vivian when she had no one.

17. **Who does this character not trust and why?**

    Vivian does not trust Edward initially, because men have always used her. She does not trust the hotel manager, because people in his position normally treat her like dirt. She doesn't trust society people, because they look down on her, too.

18. **Who will this character trust without question at the end of the story and why?**

    By the end, Vivian does trust Edward, because he cares about her and values her.

19. **Give an example of how this character will change or grow internally by the end of the story.**

    Vivian will go from being insecure and doubting her self-worth at the beginning to becoming emotionally strong enough to demand a true commitment—marriage—from Edward at the end.

20. **What will be different externally for this character at the end of the story and why?**

    Vivian will leave the life of prostitution to seek her diploma and a better life with Edward.

1. **What two or three adjectives best define this character?**
Isolated, driven, ruthless.

2. **What does this character believe about his or her Everyday World?**
Edward believes his Everyday World is neat and orderly and that most, if not all, people are driven by money.

3. **Is the character content with his or her Everyday World at the opening of the story? Why or why not?**
Edward is content with his Everyday World, because he believes that he controls his world by his ability to make money without emotional consequences.

4. **What would this character say is his or her strength?**
Edward would say his strength is being a powerful negotiator who does not let emotion cloud his decisions.

5. **What would this character say is his or her weakness?**
Edward would say he has no weakness.

6. **What do other story characters see as this character's strength?**
Both Edward's adversaries and his associates—such as the attorney—revere his business acumen, which is based on not allowing emotions to enter decision-making. Vivian sees Edward's sense of self-worth as a strength and in contrast to her own sense of worth.

7. **What do other story characters see as this character's weakness?**
Edward's attorney sees Edward's interest in Vivian as a weakness. Vivian sees Edward's inability to see the human cost of his acquisitions as a blind spot.

8. **If this character's occupation influences the story in a significant way, what is his or her occupation, and how does he or she feel about it?**

   Edward is a very successful corporate raider who loves what he does.

9. **How are you going to create (show) reader sympathy for this character in the opening of your story?**

   When his current live-in girlfriend in New York breaks up with him via phone on a very important day for him, Edward asks a former girlfriend a question about how he handles relationships. When she gives him a truthful answer he might not have wanted to hear, he tells her how lucky her new husband is to have her. He and this prior girlfriend have a warm exchange, indicating she doesn't hate him, so the viewer is willing to believe he's a decent guy.

10. **What is lacking internally for this character, even if he or she is not aware of it?**

    Edward lacks the ability to emotionally bond with another person or to be intimate, so he never has a true relationship with anyone, either in his business or his personal life.

11. **What does this character value most in life and why?**

    In the beginning of the story, Edward values power and money most in life.

12. **What do you, as the author, want as the overall External Story Goal for this character?**

    For Edward to partner with the elderly shipping businessman to begin building something rather than taking over and dismantling the struggling company.

13. **What will happen if this character does not reach his or her overall External Story Goal that you, as the author, know must be attempted?**

    Edward will continue the legacy of his father—destroying businesses and other people's lives.

14. **What does this character want externally at the beginning of the story (his or her most Immediate External Goal)?**

    Edward is driving an unfamiliar car and wants to find directions to his hotel.

15. **What will happen if this character does not reach his or her Immediate External Goal?**

Edward stands to be mugged—or worse—since he is barely capable of driving the car, and he is lost in a seedy part of Hollywood.

16. **Who does this character trust at the beginning of the story and why?**

Edward trusts no one at the beginning of the story, as he assumes all other people are motivated solely by money. As long as he continues to make money, and pay others, he will have people in his life, but not anyone he can trust.

17. **Who does this character not trust and why?**

Edward trusts no one because his own father betrayed his trust as a child.

18. **Who will this character trust without question at the end of the story and why?**

Edward will trust Vivian by the end of the story, because she has shown she has his best interest at heart even without any monetary expectation. He'll trust the grandfatherly businessman enough to form a partnership, because the grandfather shows Edward the value of building a business over dismantling one.

19. **Give an example of how this character will change or grow internally by the end of the story.**

Edward will change from an emotionally isolated man who believes all relationships come with a price tag to a man who is able to love and willing to believe there is good in people like the older businessman and that Vivian's love is real.

20. **What will be different externally for this character at the end of the story and why?**

Externally at the end, Edward will no longer take over companies to dismantle, but will now build companies and will marry Vivian.

1. **What two or three adjectives best define this character?**

   Cynical loner and politically neutral.

2. **What does this character believe about his or her Everyday World?**

   Rick believes he can keep his Everyday World safe as long as he does not get involved with anyone else's problems.

3. **Is the character content with his or her Everyday World at the opening of the story? Why or why not?**

   Rick appears content, although others in his world appear to think differently.

4. **What would this character say is his or her strength?**

   Rick would say that his strength is in being unemotional.

5. **What would this character say is his or her weakness?**

   Rick believes that his past tendency to care about others is a weakness.

6. **What do other story characters see as this character's strength?**

   Ilsa sees Rick's strength as being able to make decisions and carry them through. Captain Renault sees Rick's strength as being trustworthy, that his word is his bond.

7. **What do other story characters see as this character's weakness?**

   Renault believes Rick is still a patriot, which is a weakness in Casablanca at this time. Ilsa sees Rick's bitterness as a weakness. German Major Strasser sees Rick's idealism as a weakness.

8. **If this character's occupation influences the story in a significant way, what is his or her occupation, and how does he or she feel about it?**

   Rick likes owning a popular bar that's at the center of intrigue for those trying desperately to flee Casablanca, because he believes he's in control of his world.

9. **How are you going to create (show) reader sympathy for this character in the opening of your story?**

   All of Rick's employees talk about aspects of Rick's personality that he doesn't show such as loyalty and generosity. He also makes sure his former lover is escorted home safely when she's had too much to drink. He doesn't betray the thief who stole the Letters of Transit and gave them to Rick to keep safe.

10. **What is lacking internally for this character, even if he or she is not aware of it?**

    Rick lacks connection, because he's unable to move beyond being hurt by Ilsa. He keeps both people and political causes at arm's length, which leaves him emotionally isolated.

11. **What does this character value most in life and why?**

    Rick values privacy and no personal baggage, because he lost his belief in others when Ilsa broke his heart.

12. **What do you, as the author, want as the overall External Story Goal for this character?**

    For Rick to choose the Allied side in the war against Germany, and for Rick to help Ilsa and Laszlo escape.

13. **What will happen if this character does not reach his or her overall External Story Goal that you, as the author, know must be attempted?**

    If Rick does not choose a political side he jeopardizes Ilsa and Laszlo's lives, plus he undermines the Resistance movement.

14. **What does this character want externally at the beginning of the story (his or her most Immediate External Goal)?**

    Rick wants to remain neutral. He wants to hide the Letters of Transit, because he knows they are very valuable.

15. **What will happen if this character does not reach his or her Immediate External Goal?**

    Rick stands to be imprisoned if the Germans find out he has the Letters of Transit.

16. **Who does this character trust at the beginning of the story and why?**

    Rick only trusts Sam, his piano player, in the beginning.

17. **Who does this character not trust and why?**

    Rick trusts no one except Sam, especially Captain Renault and Major Strasser.

18. **Who will this character trust without question at the end of the story and why?**

    By the end of the story Rick will trust Ilsa, Laszlo, and Captain Renault.

19. **Give an example of how this character will change or grow internally by the end of the story.**

    Rick will go from being a cynical and emotionally void person bent on neutrality to a man who cares about people and feels love again. He is able to take up the sword to fight once more. He shows this by creating a situation that allows the Resistance leader, Laszlo, to escape with Ilsa. So though Rick found love, for the greater good he makes Ilsa leave.

20. **What will be different externally for this character at the end of the story and why?**

    Rick will no longer own his bar, and it's implied that he will return to freedom fighting.

POWERFUL CHARACTER MOVIE EXAMPLE:
Finding Nemo

THE CHARACTER FOR THIS TEMPLATE IS:
Marlin

1. **What two or three adjectives best define this character?**
   Hypersensitive and overprotective father.

2. **What does this character believe about his or her Everyday World?**
   Marlin believes everything outside his home is dangerous.

3. **Is the character content with his or her Everyday World at the opening of the story? Why or why not?**
   Marlin is content to stay in his Everyday World of his home, because that is the only way he believes he can protect his only child Nemo. He's also content to keep Nemo close to their home.

4. **What would this character say is his or her strength?**
   Marlin believes his strength is in being an ever-vigilant father by keeping his child from harm.

5. **What would this character say is his or her weakness?**
   Marlin would say that his failure once before to keep his family safe was a weakness.

6. **What do other story characters see as this character's strength?**
   Nemo believes his father's strength is that he is a good and loving father who will do anything in his power to save Nemo.

7. **What do other story characters see as this character's weakness?**
   Nemo thinks his father's weaknesses are his fear of the outside world and his unwillingness to let Nemo experience any of the outside world.

8. **If this character's occupation influences the story in a significant way, what is his or her occupation, and how does he or she feel about it?**
   Marlin does not have an occupation beyond being a single father, which is all he cares about.

9. **How are you going to create (show) reader sympathy for this character in the opening of your story?**

   By showing in the opening scene (prologue) how Marlin once was trusting and excited about life before tragedy struck, how much he loved his wife, and how they are looking forward to bringing their children into the world.

10. **What is lacking internally for this character, even if he or she is not aware of it?**

    Marlin lacks the ability to relax as a father and allow his son to experience life. He lacks confidence in his ability to protect his child and won't let Nemo take a risk of any sort.

11. **What does this character value most in life and why?**

    Marlin values his son more than anything.

12. **What do you, as the author, want as the overall External Story Goal for this character?**

    For Marlin to find Nemo and rescue him, and in the process learn to live and function in the larger world.

13. **What will happen if this character does not reach his or her overall External Story Goal that you, as the author, know must be attempted?**

    Since Nemo is Marlin's only family, if Marlin cannot rescue him, Marlin will have lost everyone who matters to him.

14. **What does this character want externally at the beginning of the story (his or her most Immediate External Goal)?**

    Marlin wants to get Nemo to school and back home as quickly and safely as possible.

15. **What will happen if this character does not reach his or her Immediate External Goal?**

    If Marlin fails, it means Nemo has been put in jeopardy, which means his worst fear has come true—that something has happened to his child.

16. **Who does this character trust at the beginning of the story and why?**

    Marlin trusts no one, not even Nemo, at the beginning, because Marlin believes that everyone is too casual about the dangers in the world.

17. **Who does this character not trust and why?**

    As noted above, Marlin trusts no one.

18. **Who will this character trust without question at the end of the story and why?**

    Marlin learns to trust others including Nemo; his new friend, Dory; the Sharks who are not eating him; and the schoolteacher who can now take Nemo off to visit the far Reef.

19. **Give an example of how this character will change or grow internally by the end of the story.**

    By the end, Marlin is willing to take a risk to save Dory rather than shy away from danger or rush Nemo back to the safety of their home. This will show that he has become a part of a larger community and capable of living.

20. **What will be different externally for this character at the end of the story and why?**

    Marlin will enjoy life outside his home, as well as have a better relationship with his son and the larger community of fish.

2 CONFLICT
Driving the Plot

> "Conflict is a clash of wants."
> —Ulf Wolf

The best way to describe conflict has been used many times over the years—two dogs, one bone. Ordinarily, with both dogs well fed, the conflict might not appear to be too strong, but what if a weather disaster has ravaged the landscape and there hasn't been food in days? Then we introduce two dogs that come upon a steak. Now you have a whole new degree of conflict. The key to this conflict is the motivation—hunger—that translates into the stronger motivation of survival.

Many manuscripts are rejected quickly due to lack of conflict. The polite reasons such as "characters weren't fully developed" or "plot wasn't big enough" or "didn't strike a chord with me" can usually be traced back to the conflict not being strong enough to drive the plot. Conflict is that important. As readers, we aren't interested in stories where everyone is happy and any conflict can be solved with a conversation (yawn . . . boring). Weaving believable conflicts—both major and minor—throughout the story in subtle to vivid ways is what keeps the reader turning pages.

In the movie *Overboard,* Goldie Hawn plays Joanna, a millionaire woman who doesn't pay Dean (Kurt Russell), a hard-working carpenter and a single father, after Joanna and Dean argue about a closet he built on her yacht. The next day Joanna hits her head and falls overboard. She is rescued by Dean, a man raising four kids alone. When Joanna awakens with amnesia, Dean sees the perfect opportunity to get the money she owes him by telling her she's his wife. He now has a housekeeper and mother. Joanna may not know her name, but she is still domestically challenged. Added to the opening conflict situation, this is a classic "fish out of water" (excuse the pun) conflict that drives the humor in the movie and the story forward.

> *For me, the hardest part of writing a book is doing my detailed outline that weaves together all the elements of the story, so I have a "book map" that makes sure no key element is left out or neglected when I sit down to do the chapters*
>
> —Haywood Smith, *New York Times* best-selling author of *The Red Hat Club* and *Wedding Belles*

There are two forms of conflict in a story—Internal and External. The external conflict should force internal change for the character over the course of the story (Internal Character Growth). Without the external conflict or "tests," the character will not change internally. The bigger the conflict, the stronger the story. In *Overboard,* if the story had only been about Joanna and Dean disagreeing over the money she owed him, the story would have fallen flat. Any reason for the two of them to interact voluntarily would have been hard to believe since the difference in their social positions gave this pair no reason to be in the same place at the same time after the argument. To make this story work, the characters had to be as polar opposites in personalities as they were in income levels.

POWER PLOTTING TIP Your character should not be able to reach his or her External Story Goal without making a major internal change. The internal change is the Internal Character Growth, or the character arc. The external conflicts comprise the story arc. True character emerges during a crisis. This doesn't mean every conflict must be a crisis, but each conflict should force the character out of his or her comfort zone to make changes in degrees. The conflicts should escalate each time leading to a climax far greater than the first conflict.

CONFLICT TEMPLATE

The purpose of this template is to determine if your characters have true conflict and how to ratchet up the conflict as the story moves forward.

The Character for this template is:

----

1. What is this character's Immediate External Goal at the beginning of the story?

----

2. What is in the way of this character reaching his or her Immediate External Goal at the beginning of the story?

----

3. Why can't this conflict be solved with a discussion? What makes this a challenge?

----

4. What is the External Story Goal you, as the author, have set for this character?

   TIP: Reference the Powerful Character Template in Chapter 1.

----

5. What is this character lacking internally (emotionally) at the beginning of your story that will change by the end of the story?

   TIP: Reference the Powerful Character Template in Chapter 1.

   ----

6. What belief system or event created this internal lack?

   ----

7. How does this lack impact others around this character initially?

   ----

8. How will the first decision and actions this character takes toward his or her Immediate External Goal impact his or her Internal Character Growth after the action is taken?

   TIP: Internal Character Growth evolves through small steps and since not all external actions cause internal change, look for an external action that will impact this character internally.

   ----

9. What will be three *significant* external obstacles to this character reaching his or her External Story Goal?

> **TIP:** These are the three twist points leading to the climax.

---

10. What will be three *significant* internal changes to this character as a result of overcoming external obstacles that will allow the character to reach his or her Internal Character Growth?

> **TIP:** Sometimes the internal change happens in order to accomplish the external decision/action or sometimes the result of an external action causes the internal change to happen.

The Bourne Identity

THE CHARACTER FOR THIS TEMPLATE IS:
Jason Bourne (Matt Damon)

1. **What is this character's Immediate External Goal at the beginning of the story?**

   Jason's goal is to find clues to his identity; he plans to accomplish this by using the numbers in the capsule taken from his hip to access the bank vault in Switzerland.

2. **What is in the way of this character reaching his or her Immediate External Goal at the beginning of the story?**

   Although Jason arrives in Switzerland and accesses the vault, the information he finds creates more questions and the visit puts him in immediate danger.

3. **Why can't this conflict be solved with a discussion? What makes this a challenge?**

   Because rather than producing answers about his prior life, the material Jason finds in the safe-deposit box creates more questions and points at a dark past. Once he's being chased, Jason also doesn't know who is after him, so he can't have a discussion with anyone. As he realizes he's been trained to be some kind of elite warrior he starts to realize there may be many reasons for someone to want to stop him.

4. **What is the External Story Goal you, as the author, have set for this character?**

   Jason will have to face the CIA individuals who trained him and stop their actions.

5. **What is this character lacking internally (emotionally) at the beginning of your story that will change by the end of the story?**

   Jason lacks the ability to trust and connect with others.

6. **What belief system or event created this internal lack?**

    Because at some prior time he was trained as an assassin—a life where survival depends on having no true connection or attachment with anyone.

7. **How does this lack impact others around this character initially?**

    While this lack of attachment keeps him alive as an assassin, it also prevents him from any emotional connection. His amnesia has allowed him to realize—deep down—that connection is something he wants to have. But once others discover he's been an assassin, they hesitate to get involved with him.

8. **How will the first decision and actions this character takes toward his or her Immediate External Goal impact his or her Internal Character Growth after the action is taken?**

    What Jason discovers in the Swiss safe-deposit box makes him aware that he has lived a life of lies. This takes him one step closer to facing that what he did is not who he is now—and a choice will have to be made: return to who and what he was in the past or re-create himself in the future.

9. **What will be three *significant* external obstacles to this character reaching his or her External Story Goal?**

    An African leader has been assassinated and Jason is being set up as the assassin. When Jason has to kill the assassin who has been sent to kill him, the assassin gives Jason insight into who he is (an equal assassin) and who is after him. Then Jason figures out he must fight the Treadstone organization in Paris.

10. **What will be three *significant* internal changes to this character as a result of overcoming external obstacles that will allow the character to reach his or her Internal Character Growth?**

    Due to being set up for the African leader's death, Jason realizes he was trained as an assassin. After facing an assassin sent to kill him, Jason realizes he has to choose to use his abilities to stop the people after him. Once he faces the Treadstone group and tells them he's done with the agency and walks away, Jason believes he can be free.

1. **What is this character's Immediate External Goal at the beginning of the story?**

   Vivian's Immediate External Goal is to make enough money to pay her rent.

2. **What is in the way of this character reaching his or her Immediate External Goal at the beginning of the story?**

   Vivian meets a man who clearly does not pay hookers for company.

3. **Why can't this conflict be solved with a discussion? What makes this a challenge?**

   Vivian is barely able to talk Edward, a wealthy and attractive man, into paying her a few bucks for directions, much less sex.

4. **What is the External Story Goal you, as the author, have set for this character?**

   Vivian is to walk away from being a prostitute for a better life.

5. **What is this character lacking internally (emotionally) at the beginning of your story that will change by the end of the story?**

   Vivian lacks a strong sense of self worth.

6. **What belief system or event created this internal lack?**

   Vivian believes her poor choices in men is why she is destitute, far from home and facing a dismal future as a hooker to survive. This has completely destroyed any confidence she had in herself; that is why she doesn't trust what any man offers her beyond money for a night.

7. **How does this lack impact others around this character initially?**

This lack makes it easy for others to take advantage of Vivian's good nature—like her roommate spending the rent money on drugs. Vivian's lack of confidence means letting others use her. She let men use her in the past, and now, she is letting them use her sexually in exchange for money.

8. **How will the first decision and actions this character takes toward his or her Immediate External Goal impact his or her Internal Character Growth after the action is taken?**

Once Vivian has her most immediate cash need met by staying with Edward for one night, it's easier for her to negotiate and accept his offer to have her stay for a week, which will impact her self-image.

9. **What will be three *significant* external obstacles to this character reaching his or her External Story Goal?**

Getting someone to sell Vivian clothes and convincing someone to show her how to eat properly in a fancy restaurant; Edward's attorney finds out that she is a hooker and he uses that information to remind her she's only pretending to be a respectable woman; when Vivian leaves Edward after he offers her only a long-term paid arrangement (her leaving is the obstacle to reaching her External Story Goal of security, because if she stayed she would have security; but at the end she is no longer willing to accept exchanging money for sex).

10. **What will be three *significant* internal changes to this character as a result of overcoming external obstacles that will allow the character to reach his or her Internal Character Growth?**

Once Vivian dons the new clothes she starts to feel like a better person; when the attorney embarrasses her, Vivian realizes she wants to be treated as a respected partner, especially by Edward; once Vivian turns down Edward's offer, she is not willing to accept less than being treated as his equal.

1. **What is this character's Immediate External Goal at the beginning of the story?**

    To find directions to his hotel.

2. **What is in the way of this character reaching his or her Immediate External Goal at the beginning of the story?**

    He is normally driven around in a limousine, so he doesn't know the streets and he is driving an unfamiliar car, which is a stick shift.

3. **Why can't this conflict be solved with a discussion? What makes this a challenge?**

    While he might get directions in a discussion, he still cannot drive the car.

4. **What is the External Story Goal you, as the author, have set for this character?**

    To build businesses rather than tear them apart.

5. **What is this character lacking internally (emotionally) at the beginning of your story that will change by the end of the story?**

    Edward lacks an ability to emotionally connect with other people and trust them.

6. **What belief system or event created this internal lack?**

    Edward's father abandoned him and his mother for a better deal (another woman), so Edward's belief is that emotions don't enter into decisions. As a consequence, Edward lacks the ability to care about how his actions affect others personally.

7. **How does this lack impact others around this character initially?**

   Edward's lack of caring has left a string of ex-girlfriends who felt ignored. Also, his lack of caring is tearing apart the grandfatherly businessman who has given all for his company and employees. And Edward's lack of ability to care is keeping him from accepting that he wants more from Vivian than a monetary relationship.

8. **How will the first decision and actions this character takes toward his or her Immediate External Goal impact his or her Internal Character Growth after the action is taken?**

   The decision to let Vivian ride with him rather than just give him directions results in Edward making the first step toward his internal change by allowing her to drive the car to the hotel. This shows a minimum trust of her.

9. **What will be three *significant* obstacles to this character reaching his or her External Story Goal?**

   In spite of his initial admiration of the grandfatherly businessman, Edward must redouble his efforts to take over the man's business; Edward's jealous reaction to Vivian flirting with the grandson of the business owner at the polo match; when Vivian refuses Edward's offer to become his mistress and leaves.

10. **What will be three *significant* internal changes to this character as a result of overcoming external obstacles that will allow the character to reach his or her Internal Character Growth?**

    As a result of Vivian's influence, Edward is starting to feel twinges of emotions in business dealings; after having reacted to Vivian's flirting at the polo match, Edward realizes he must apologize to keep Vivian around; when Vivian refuses to accept his arrangement, Edward realizes he has to risk emotionally to keep her forever.

1. **What is this character's Immediate External Goal at the beginning of the story?**

   To remain neutral in the war between Germany and most of Europe and North Africa.

2. **What is in the way of this character reaching his or her Immediate External Goal at the beginning of the story?**

   Agreeing to hide the Letters of Transit causes a kink in Rick's plan to remain neutral when Ilsa, his former lover, and her husband, a resistance fighter Rick has always admired, show up at his bar in desperate need of those papers to escape.

3. **Why can't this conflict be solved with a discussion? What makes this a challenge?**

   If Rick admits to having the Letters of Transit, he puts himself and all his staff at risk.

4. **What is the External Story Goal you, as the author, have set for this character?**

   To choose a side in the war plus help Ilsa and Laszlo escape.

5. **What is this character lacking internally (emotionally) at the beginning of your story that will change by the end of the story?**

   Due to getting his heart broken in Paris by Ilsa, Rick decided to become emotionally neutral with regard to all parts of his life. By the end of the story, Rick will once again care about people and the resistance movement.

6. **What belief system or event created this internal lack?**

   Rick believes if he remains neutral on everything—people, world issues—he can prevent himself from ever getting hurt again and remain safe in Casablanca.

7. **How does this lack impact others around this character initially?**

The thief gave Rick the Letter of Transit papers. The thief felt the papers would be safe with Rick, because he knew Rick did not get involved with anyone.

8. **How will the first decision and actions this character takes toward his or her Immediate External Goal impact his or her Internal Character Growth after the action is taken?**

Rick's decision to talk with Ilsa, instead of remaining neutral, creates strong emotions in him. Mostly bitter, angry feelings, but even so these are emotions and feeling them starts his healing process.

9. **What will be three *significant* external obstacles to this character reaching his or her External Story Goal?**

When Ilsa, the woman who he once loved, shows up in Rick's bar needing the Letters of Transit in Rick's possession; Laszlo puts Rick on the spot to make a choice when Laszlo encourages the French to sing their national anthem louder than the Germans; Rick holds a gun on Captain Renault while Laszlo and Ilsa flee.

10. **What will be three *significant* internal changes to this character as a result of overcoming external obstacles that will allow the character to reach his or her Internal Character Growth?**

When Ilsa shows up, Rick realizes he can no longer pretend he doesn't feel anything about Ilsa; when Laszlo puts Rick on the spot with the French singing against the Germans, Rick realizes he does support the French and the Resistance movement; when Rick holds the gun on Captain Renault, he realizes he loves Ilsa enough to let her go and he cares about the Resistance movement enough to help Laszlo escape.

1. **What is this character's Immediate External Goal at the beginning of the story?**

   To protect Nemo from all threats and prevent him from taking risks, which includes attending school and swimming around in the larger, more frightening ocean.

2. **What is in the way of this character reaching his or her Immediate External Goal at the beginning of the story?**

   When Marlin is unable to stop Nemo from attending school, Nemo is abducted by a fish collector and taken away.

3. **Why can't this conflict be solved with a discussion? What makes this a challenge?**

   The only way Marlin can protect Nemo now is to find him and rescue him.

4. **What is the External Story Goal you, as the author, have set for this character?**

   Marlin's external goal is to rescue Nemo.

5. **What is this character lacking internally (emotionally) at the beginning of your story that will change by the end of the story?**

   Marlin lacks a sense of security for himself and his son, limiting Marlin and Nemo from experiencing life fully.

6. **What belief system or event created this internal lack?**

   Marlin's wife and all his children except Nemo were killed by a predator fish because Marlin was unable to protect them. Then Marlin started assuming that only his vigilance and overprotectiveness would keep such an event from happening again.

7. **How does this lack impact others around this character initially?**

Marlin's fears keep him and Nemo isolated. This isolation limits Nemo's experience of the world, which he is eager to explore. This isolation also keeps both of them from being part of a larger fish community of neighbors, friends, and more.

8. **How will the first decision and actions this character takes toward his or her Immediate External Goal impact his or her Internal Character Growth after the action is taken?**

Because Marlin is forced to swim into the larger ocean to try and find Nemo, he must face his fears and limitations. One of the first limitations he faces is his isolation. Then he finds Dory, who not only gives him hope that he's swimming in the right direction, but is willing to go along with him to help.

9. **What will be three *significant* external obstacles to this character reaching his or her External Story Goal?**

Marlin encounters Dory and must act in spite of his fear; Marlin must trust Dory's instincts when they are swallowed by a whale that this is not a bad thing; Marlin faces having to rescue Dory when she is caught in a commercial fishing net.

10. **What will be three *significant* internal changes to this character as a result of overcoming external obstacles that will allow the character to reach his or her Internal Character Growth?**

In accepting Dory's help, Marlin realizes he does need other fish (people); once Marlin trusted Dory inside the whale, he realized that sometimes good can come out of bad situations; as a result of saving Dory from being caught in the net, Marlin realized that living life fully was sometimes about taking risks for others.

3 POWER OPENINGS
Grab Them by the Throat

> *The beginning of a plot is the prompting of desire*
> —Christopher Lehmann-Haupt

When a reader opens a book you have less than thirty seconds to grab his or her attention. You have to anchor readers quickly and answer the question: Why should they buy and read this book?

We don't particularly care about peaceful settings or happy worlds that don't change right away. This doesn't mean your story has to open with guns blazing and people in danger, but you must show the reader quickly why your story opens with that POV character in that specific setting at that specific moment. If your story starts in a peaceful setting, then you should be considering how to disrupt that peace.

For example: If the opening scene is of a woman (POV character) strolling out to her mailbox in a quiet and happy suburbia, smiling and waving at neighbors as she stops to pull out her mail; then something in her mail should throw a major kink into her world to disrupt the peaceful setting. This would show us immediately that either her world is an illusion or that her worst nightmare has just come true. Now we're interested in reading further.

I like to start my stories in media res, which is Latin for in the middle of things. This technique puts the story's conflict at the start of the story.

—Roland Haas, best-selling author of *Enter the Past Tense: My Secret Life as a CIA Assassin*

There are two ways to approach your opening and using both is better than one. The first way is to consider everything the reader absolutely needs to know in that opening scene. Don't build a shopping list opening, but do use this list to see if you might be missing something important that the reader needs to know:

Setting: Be specific and decide what will anchor the reader without bogging down the pacing.

An intriguing situation: The opening has to pique the reader's curiosity, create questions, and tap into an emotion.

Create an Immediate External Goal with a *ticking clock*: This creates a sense of urgency to turn the page.

Plausible and strong character motivation to reach the Immediate External Goal: This is where the reader begins to bond with the character. If the character is not motivated to act, the action taken will either come across as contrived or unimportant. If it is contrived, the reader will be disappointed before they get started. If the motivation to act is not important to the character, then it's not important to the reader.

Scene opens with a strong *hook* and ends on a better one: The opening creates a question and the end of the scene leaves the reader with even more questions.

Dialogue: Conversation is an active way to start a story if the conversation serves a purpose in hooking the reader.

The second way of looking at your opening scene is by purging whatever is not absolutely necessary in the scene.

Back Story that has no bearing on the opening scene: For example, if in the opening scene a man is trying to disarm a bomb, we don't really need to know that he's married or divorced any more than we need to know if he had a happy or miserable childhood.

Setting: Take all the setting description out of the scene and paste those lines in a separate document. See if any of this information could be condensed down or deleted if it is redundant. Prioritize each sentence by significance and why that line must be at *this* point in the story.

Dialogue: Conversation should not be mundane chatter just to introduce two or more people.

Introspection: Thoughts can sound active and engaging or come across as information dumps, especially if the story opens with several pages of introspection. The more action you weave through the introspection, the easier to pull the reader into the scene, and thus into the story.

In the following scene from *Out of Control,* author Suzanne Brockmann opens in Kenny "Wildcard" Karmody's POV. He's a protagonist (one of two since this is a romantic suspense), and this particular series is about Navy SEALs. The opening line is:

> At about 0530 that very morning, Ken "Wildcard" Karmody became a terrorist.
>
> It wasn't a career move he would normally have made, especially on such short notice, with no time to prepare properly. But seeing how it was a direct order, he had no choice but to embrace it completely.

Even without knowing the protagonist is a SEAL, the word choice of "0530" for time and "career move" plus "a direct order" clues the reader in quickly that this person is in the military. We want to know why he was ordered to be a terrorist, what he is going to do and how he feels about this order. As you read further down the page, you realize he's on a training op and is clearly planning to break the rules on this op, which could get him in deep trouble. But we're interested in seeing if his team wins against the British SAS agency, and how they'll do it. Within the first few paragraphs, we get a quick insight into the internal issues for this character when, after Kenny has told a captured Scottish SAS officer named Gordon that he has to strip. Gordon is ticked off (in Kenny's POV).

> [Gordon is talking] "Kenneth. Be reasonable lad. It's a training op. You're only supposed to *pretend* to be the bad guys. Don't you know if you let my boys catch you and liberate me, you'll be home in your girlfriend's bed before 2230?"
>
> His girlfriend's bed.
>
> The rest of the SEALs who were playing the part of Ken's merry band of nasties got very quiet. Too quiet.
>
> What, did they honestly think those three words—*his* and *girlfriend's* and *bed*—would set him off? He could feel their uncertainty bouncing around the rough-hewn walls of the shack.
>
> Yup. No doubt about it.

Suzanne Brockmann does a great job of opening in an interesting way that shows the character and introduces his internal issues plus giving you setting while never slowing the pace. Use the following template to fine-tune your opening scene, then study openings of books you bought (not those that were given to you) to see what made you buy those books.

POWERFUL OPENINGS TEMPLATE

The purpose of this template is to determine if your story opens in an engaging way and at the right spot. Use this to analyze why other openings work (or don't work) and to strengthen your story opening.

POV Character for this template is:

----

1. What is this character's significance to the opening of your story?

----

2. Where is this character physically in the opening scene and why is this specific setting important?

----

3. What details are you going to share about the character and why?

----

4. Why are these details necessary right now (what do the details show?) and what is the ticking clock?

----

5. Why do we care about this character or the future of this character?

----

6. Is there any unnecessary information that is slowing the opening?

----

7. What question(s) will this opening create? What are the hooks that will compel the reader to continue reading?

> **TIP:** This is what you are going for.

----

8. What emotional stakes (fear, excitement, tension, etc.) are raised at the beginning and how does this emotion foreshadow your story?

POWER PLOTTING TIP There is no perfect opening for any story, but there are several potential strong ones and just as many potentially boring ones. Your job is to drop us into the story at the moment when a character's life is about to change drastically. Think "forward movement" when you think "opening," instead of events that have happened in the past. If you find that too much of your opening is in the past tense, you are probably in Back Story and you need to start your opening at a different point.

1. **What is this character's significance to the opening of your story?**

    Opening scene main character is Jason Bourne. His significance to the story is that the entire story revolves around finding out his true identity.

2. **Where is this character physically in the opening scene and why is this specific setting important?**

    Jason is pulled aboard a commercial fishing boat in the Mediterranean Sea, south of Marseilles in France, and he has amnesia. Regaining consciousness with friendly commercial fishermen allows Jason a safe place to heal from the gunshot wounds in his back and to try to figure out what happened to him and who he is without facing unknown threats.

3. **What details are you going to share about the character and why?**

    If he was shot in the back, we assume he was either being chased by dangerous people or was fleeing a dangerous situation, but we don't know if he's a good guy or a bad guy. The minute he comes to, Jason's immediate defensive reflex shows a hint of his skills. The opening also shows he knows some things, such as how to read nautical characters, tie knots, and speak several languages without knowing who he was or why he was shot.

4. **Why are these details necessary right now (what do these details show?) and what is the ticking clock?**

    Showing that he has been shot twice and has no memory of anything before being rescued sets up an imminent threat that someone wants Jason dead. The longer it takes him to figure out his identity, the slimmer his chances of survival.

5. **Why do we care about this character or the future of this character?**

Because we see Jason through the eyes of the
fishermen; they are unbiased men who take care of
Jason as he heals. We care about Jason because we
feel for a person with amnesia who is alone. We can
empathize with his frustration and concerns.

6. **Is there any unnecessary information that is slowing the opening?**

There is no unnecessary information slowing the
opening. Every movement and line used drives the story
forward.

7. **What question(s) will this opening create? What are the hooks that will compel the reader to continue reading?**

The questions created are: Who is Jason? Can he regain
his memory? Why was he shot? Who wants him dead? The
hooks are: two bullet holes in his back, his amnesia,
and a capsule imbedded in his hip with the number of a
Swiss safe-deposit box.

8. **What emotional stakes are raised at the beginning and how does this emotion foreshadow your story?**

The emotional stakes for Jason are fear of never
discovering who he is and the tension of who wants him
dead. This foreshadows the events that will unfold
as he pushes to learn his identity while fighting to
survive.

1. **What is this character's significance to the opening of your story?**

   Vivian is the protagonist, also known as the heroine, because this is a romance.

2. **Where is this character physically in the opening scene and why is this specific setting important?**

   > **TIP:** In a romance both the hero and heroine have opening scenes. After sneaking out of her seedy apartment to avoid the landlord collecting rent, Vivian is working as a cheap hooker on Hollywood Boulevard at night. This shows how precarious Vivian's Everyday World is. It also shows the contrast with Edward's more secure and affluent world.

3. **What details are you going to share about the character and why?**

   We learn that Vivian's roommate has spent Vivian's stash of rent money and that the rent is due, which shows her desperate situation. She's shown pinning her boot together with a safety pin, hiding her hair beneath a wig, escaping through a back window and walking past where a dead hooker was found before heading to her own work as a hooker—all showing how precarious her life is.

4. **Why are these details necessary right now (what do the details show?) and what is the ticking clock?**

   It's important to know that Vivian has to make a deal for that night because rent money is due—the ticking clock. All the other scene details show how marginal her survival is.

5. **Why do we care about this character or the future of this character?**

   Vivian is vulnerable to people like the drug lord if she and her roommate cannot make their rent, which puts her in a desperate position—something anyone, especially a single woman, can identify with.

6. **Is there any unnecessary information that is slowing the opening?**

    This movie has no unnecessary actions or dialogue.

7. **What question(s) will this opening create? What are the hooks that will compel the reader to continue reading?**

    The question raised is: Will Edward take her inside once they reach the hotel so she can make the money she needs? The hooks that compel us to read further are wondering how she will get the money she needs and if she can convince a wealthy man who seems only interested in directions to pay her for sex.

8. **What emotional stakes are raised at the beginning and how does this emotion foreshadow your story?**

    The emotional stake is fear, which foreshadows the insecurity of Vivian's world.

1. **What is this character's significance to the opening of your story?**

   Edward is the POV character in the opening scene, because he is the hero and this is a romance. His scene is first because this is more his story than Vivian's, since he has the greater internal Character Growth.

2. **Where is this character physically in the opening scene and why is this specific setting important?**

   Edward is at the Beverly Hills home of his attorney who has thrown a party in Edward's honor. This setting is important to establish Edward's Everyday World, to show he's surrounded by a hundred people on a very important day—except his live-in girlfriend in New York who did not attend and breaks up with him over the phone. However, no one even notices when he leaves.

3. **What details are you going to share about the character and why?**

   We learn that Edward is now unattached and that, although he's brilliant in business, he fails at personal relationships. We learn that when he wants something, he's used to being able to buy it. whether it's directions, help driving a manual transmission car, or for simple companionship.

4. **Why are these details necessary right now (what do these details show?) and what is the ticking clock?**

   These details are important to show how he's totally alone. A wealthy man driving an unfamiliar car in seedy areas is at risk of being a target of violence. The ticking clock is that he plans to leave Los Angeles at the end of the week.

5. **Why do we care about this character or the future of this character?**

Edward is dumped by his live-in girlfriend on an important night, but we care about him when he politely asks a former girlfriend if she talked to his secretary more than him when they were together. She replies that his secretary was her bridesmaid. Edward is very sweet when he tells the former girlfriend her new husband is a lucky man, showing that Edward is a nice guy; just remote emotionally in relationships.

6. **Is there any unnecessary information that is slowing the opening?**

No, everything in the opening—even the coin trick showing the illusion of money—plays a part.

7. **What question(s) will this opening create? What are the hooks that will compel the reader to continue reading?**

Will Edward reach his hotel safely? Will a lonely millionaire invite a streetwalker up to his penthouse?

8. **What emotional stakes are raised at the beginning and how does this emotion foreshadow your story?**

The emotional stake raised is that Edward is questioning his ability to connect with another person, specifically a woman. This lack of ability to connect foreshadows why he will be willing to take a prostitute up to his hotel room and offer her a deal to stay for a week.

1. **What is this character's significance to the opening of your story?**

    The main character in the opening is Rick and his significance is as the protagonist.

2. **Where is this character physically in the opening scene and why is this specific setting important?**

    In the opening scene for the movie (not the omniscient setup with the narrator talking that serves as back story), Rick is in his bar, Rick's Café, in the Moroccan city of Casablanca. The place is a nest of black-market deals. Also, this is Rick's Everyday World where he's totally in control in his own self-made kingdom.

3. **What details are you going to share about the character and why?**

    We'll learn that Rick drinks with no one and plays chess alone, showing how he's determined to remain neutral and aloof, with no emotional ties to anyone and no political agenda. We quickly see how cynical Rick is about everything.

4. **Why are these details necessary right now (what do they show?) and what is the ticking clock?**

    These details show Rick's internal and external conflict: He doesn't want to get involved, but ends up with the stolen set of Letters of Transit that are invaluable to those trying to escape the Nazis. When the man who gave Rick the papers to keep for him is arrested; there's an intense search for the documents. The ticking clock starts and only speeds up once Rick is faced with a former lover needing documents to escape.

continued

5. **Why do we care about this character or the future of this character?**

We care about Rick because he is a loner who seems to only want to run his bar and doesn't want to get involved. However, when Rick has a chance to save his life and hand over the papers, he doesn't do so or tell the Germans the man they arrested had stolen the papers. Also we're shown that Rick's employees are very loyal and see more in him than he sees in himself.

6. **Is there any unnecessary information that is slowing the opening?**

The opening would be tightened if shot today, because there is unnecessary information such as Rick's employee practicing English with the German couple.

7. **What question(s) will this opening create? What is (are) the hook(s) that will compel the reader to continue reading?**

The hook is: Once Rick has the Letters of Transit and Ilsa arrives needing those documents, we wonder what he's going to do.

8. **What emotional stakes are raised at the beginning and how does this emotion foreshadow your story?**

By the end of the opening scene, Rick can't ignore the significance of the Letters of Transit when Ilsa arrives, which throws him into emotional turmoil. Sitting with her to have a drink foreshadows his reconnecting with people.

1. **What is this character's significance to the opening of your story?**

   Marlin (Nemo's dad) is the main character/protagonist in the opening scene—which happens to be a prologue—because this is his story. He's the one who will grow and change the most over the course of the story.

2. **Where is this character physically in the opening scene and why is this specific setting important?**

   In the prologue, Marlin is in his anemone home with his wife and a nest of eggs when a predator attacks, kills his wife and all but one egg, which Marlin swears to watch over. In the opening scene, Marlin is in his home as well, which is important because home is the only place Marlin feels that he can protect Nemo from threats.

3. **What details are you going to share about the character and why?**

   Marlin is overprotective to an extreme degree, fearing anything beyond his home and especially the reef, but he has reasons for his fears because there are dangerous predatory fish around. This is important because the story is about Marlin learning how to expand his and Nemo's boundaries, so they can live a full life.

4. **Why are these details necessary right now (what do they show?) and what is the ticking clock?**

   It's important to know why Marlin is overprotective, because this sets up "what is the worst that can happen?" The worst is that Nemo will be in danger. When Nemo is grabbed by a diver, the urgency—ticking clock—is to find and save Nemo.

5. **Why do we care about this character or the future of this character?**

   Because anyone can feel for a man who lost his wife and all his children but one. We know Marlin should allow Nemo more freedom, but we understand his fear.

6. **Is there any unnecessary information that is slowing the opening?**

   Everything introduced is necessary to set up the story and explain why Marlin is so overprotective, and why he'll do anything to protect his only child.

7. **What question(s) will this opening create? What is (are) the hook(s) that will compel the reader to continue reading?**

   The questions/hooks are: What will happen to Nemo? How will a father who is terrified of the ocean and all the risks in it get his child back?

8. **What emotional stakes are raised at the beginning and how does this emotion foreshadow your story?**

   The emotional stake raised at the opening is Marlin's fear of losing his only child and foreshadows what he'll face emotionally over the course of the story.

Part II
STRUCTURE—POWER PLOTTING

Everyday World
Premise Stated
Seeds of Change—Pros and Cons
Momentum—Decision—Push
Action Taken—Twist Point One
Secondary Story Initiated—Test Your Premise
Things Are about to Get Far Worse
Stakes Raised—Twist Point Two
Aftermath—Regrouping/Decision
Transformation—Twist Point Three
Wins and Losses—Lessons Learned and Shared

As a writer, your plot is the structure by which all the other elements of a story—character, dialogue, pacing, conflict, etc.—will hang together.

As readers, when we read great stories, the author's work to craft the plot becomes almost invisible in that a wonderful plot allows the story to spring to life and all the other elements to shine. Neglect the power of plot and your story risks never capturing an agent's, an editor's, or a reader's attention.

These templates are designed to walk you point by point through the sections of your plot. The initial few templates will help you clarify overall story goals and intention, and allow you to make sure these elements remain consistent and true throughout your story. The middle set of templates build and develop all the elements necessary to reach the final templates where all the individual threads—character growth, conflicts, goals—are reached and resolved in a way that satisfies readers and makes them hungry to read your next book.

Building a book is a process, so don't be surprised to discover that answers to the later templates send you back to the initial ones for more depth and layering. And that you'll be referencing earlier templates in this book on Character and Conflict to fill in the Plot questions.

Feel free to use the templates for all the primary characters in your story, even if the answer for each question does not translate directly to the pages. For a romance, such as *Pretty Woman*, you'll want to use a minimum of two sets of templates, one for the heroine and one for the hero.

We've chosen to use four different movies to show you how these questions can be applied to any commercial fiction project.

According to Roget's Thesaurus, **everyday** means "Daily; usual; common; habitual."

4 POWER PLOTTING
Everyday World

> "It's important to know where a character is starting from in [his or her] Everyday World to know how [his or her] world changes by the end of [his or her] story journey."
> —Pat White, author of *Ring Around My Heart*

The Everyday World of the opening of the story is a key clue to a number of important elements for your reader. One of the largest elements is as a reference point, an anchoring for you to show characterization of not only your main character but of the character's relationships with others around him or her. The intention of showing your character acting or behaving one way in his or her Everyday World is to show change and contrast by the end of your story after the series of story events have impacted and created character growth.

Think of the character Scrooge at the beginning and ending of *A Christmas Carol*. Think of Bridget Jones in *Bridget Jones's Diary* (Renée Zellweger in the movie version) or the Jason Nesmith character (Tim Allen) in the movie *Galaxy Quest*. In each of these examples, where the characters returns to their Everyday Worlds by the end of the story we can see that they have not only grown and changed, but that their relationships have changed, too, thus making their whole world a better place. However, even if a character does not return to the Everyday

World, the author must show the character is different by the end of the story.

Another function of the Everyday World is to set up a series of Story Questions, such as why the Everyday World of Riddick in *Chronicles of Riddick* is so desolate. Only later do you find out that he's isolated himself in order to protect a young girl.

Everyday World is not to be confused with Back Story. Back Story gives the reader insights and motivation for why this particular character acts or reacts as he or she does, based on a past event or events. It should be filtered into your story in small doses or as twists to the primary story line.

If you choose to use a Prologue, this often shows the inciting incident, a catalyst that puts the story into motion from a specific incident in the character's past. The prologue most often involves only the protagonist or villain, but not always. The prologue is considered your story opening and should not be used as an information dump to get back story stated. The prologue should be an inciting incident that occurred a significant amount of time prior to when you shift to the protagonist's Everyday World in the first chapter.

Sometimes the Everyday World shows an inciting incident that foreshadows what is at stake for your character if he or she does not choose to act. In the *Chronicles of Riddick*, the inciting incident is watching the Necromongers (villains) leave a planet, destroying it completely behind them. This is a foreshadowing of the ultimate threat that will happen if the character Riddick does not help the people of the next planet in the path of the Necromongers.

Another Everyday World function (that is known by the author, but not necessarily the POV character) is to set up a character's External Story Goal or Internal Character Growth. The story characters Scrooge, Bridget Jones, and Jason Nesmith were not aware that they needed to have Internal Character Growth. Of the three of them only Bridget Jones had a clear External Story Goal at the beginning of her story (to have a solid relationship with a certain kind of man), but Scrooge and Jason Nesmith were both okay with their external lives as well as how they behaved and treated others. Through the actions of the external story, the author of these last two stories showed the character's behavior in their Everyday World to clue the audience into why the characters needed Internal Character Growth.

One last element that is vital to establish in the Everyday World is to create reader empathy with your protagonist. Empathy does not necessarily mean liking the character as much as relating to or understanding the character. One way to show this is to show loss. Many romance novels use a wounded hero or heroine, one who's lost loved ones or experienced great pain because of doing his or her job, as a way to create reader empathy for a character that may not be acting heroic in the opening of a story. In the books *Out of Control,* *Phantom in the Night,* and *Dance with the Devil,* you have wounded heroes with strong reader empathy without explaining the Back Story immediately in the Everyday World. However, each protagonist is introduced in a way that shows the reader why that character's attitude and/or actions are justified, making the reader empathize with the character.

> *Hands down I love to plot,*
> *from the first scene to the last*
> *sentence.*
>
> —Rhonda Pollero, *USA Today*
> best-selling author of the Finley
> Anderson Tanner mysteries

The intention of this template is to make sure your protagonist's Everyday World is clear to the reader and that the opening scene acts as a reference point to show character growth and change for your protagonist. If you are using this template for secondary characters—such as an Antagonist or Villain—they may not experience Internal Character Growth over the course of the story, but you'll still want to make sure these characters's motivations and Immediate External Goal conflicts with the protagonist's.

The Protagonist is the character who will be shown to have the most Internal Character Growth. If you have multiple protagonists (such as in a romance or multicharacter story), one Protagonist will change the most and the other(s) will change in lesser degrees to clue the reader into whose story is being told.

EVERYDAY WORLD

The purpose of this template is to establish a reference point for your character and show that there will be major change by the end of the story.

The Character for this template is:

----

1. When your story opens, what is this character doing and why?

----

2. What is this character's expectation of what the future will bring?

----

3. What is this character feeling internally (emotionally)?

----

4. What event or action is about to happen to this character externally that will start the character toward his or her External Story Goal?

    TIP: What is about to happen most immediately in the opening scene that you as the author know, since the character may or may not?

----

5. What is the ticking clock?

> **TIP:** A "ticking clock" is an internal or external element in the story that creates a limit to how much time the character has to complete his or her Immediate External Goal.

----

6. What is the overall (to the end) External Story Goal planned for this character that you as the author know, even if your character may be unaware of it?

----

7. How will this character's External Story Goal impact his or her Internal Character Growth by the end of your story or how will this character's Internal Character Growth impact his or her External Story Goal?

----

8. Who are the key people present in this character's Everyday World?

----

9. What other significant characters will be in your story?

----

10. Describe (show) three details (internal or external) about this character that will change over the course of the story.

POWER PLOTTING TIP Your character's Everyday World is the world they are in at the beginning of chapter one. Focus on the details (a room, a town, a universe, a boat in the ocean) that define your main character's Everyday World. In *Cinderella*, her Everyday World was scrubbing floors in the home of her stepmother. In *Star Wars*, Luke Skywalker's Everyday World was on another planet, but still in a remote farming area. In the original *Spider-Man*, Peter Parker is a teen whose Everyday World is his bedroom and high school.

Jason's Everyday World is floating in the Mediterranean Sea with amnesia.

1. **When your story opens, what is this character doing and why?**

   Jason's unconscious body is being fished out of the icy storm-tossed Mediterranean Sea by fishermen. When he comes to awareness, he is suffering from amnesia and finds that a capsule is imbedded beneath his skin with the number of a Swiss safe-deposit box.

2. **What is this character's expectation of what the future will bring?**

   Not much. It appears Jason's been shot, but he doesn't know why.

3. **What is this character feeling internally (emotionally)?**

   Jason feels adrift, confused. Determined to find answers.

4. **What event or action is about to happen to this character externally that will start the character toward his or her External Story Goal?**

   Most immediately, once Jason is put ashore, he's going to go to Switzerland and find out about the safe-deposit box.

5. **What is the ticking clock?**

   Jason is desperate to learn who he is and what happened to him. Then the police start chasing him, because he attacks two of them when they roust him out of a Swiss park. Later, he trips international security alerts.

6. **What is the overall (to the end) External Story Goal planned for this character that you as the author know, even if your character may be unaware of it?**

   Jason's overall External Story Goal is to stop Treadstone, even though in the beginning he doesn't know they exist.

7. **How will this character's External Story Goal impact his or her Internal Character Growth by the end of your story or how will this character's Internal Character Growth impact his or her External Story Goal?**

   Stopping Treadstone is vital for Jason to discover who he really is now as a person.

8. **Who are the key people present in this character's Everyday World?**

   No one that Jason knows personally. As far as he's concerned, he's totally alone.

9. **What other significant characters will be in your story?**

   Marie. His CIA handler.

10. **Describe (show) three details (internal or external) about this character that will change over the course of the story.**

    Jason realizes he knows things, but not why he knows them. For instance, he can tie sailor's knots but doesn't have the calluses of a sailor. He has an innate distrust of strangers; i.e., when the Swiss police approach him while he is sleeping on a bench, his instinctive reaction is to overpower and neutralize them. Jason shares information with no one, such as not telling the fishermen who saved his life what he plans to do next.

Vivian's Everyday World is working as a prostitute on Hollywood Boulevard.

1. **When your story opens, what is this character doing and why?**

   Vivian is figuring out a way to make the rent money, because Vivian's roommate squandered all Vivian's stashed money.

2. **What is this character's expectation of what the future will bring?**

   Vivian expects life to be precarious and lurch from day to day insecurely.

3. **What is this character feeling internally (emotionally)?**

   Exasperated. Resigned.

4. **What event or action is about to happen to this character externally that will start the character toward his or her External Story Goal?**

   Most immediately, Vivian is going out to turn a few tricks as the quickest way to make some money. She's about to meet wealthy Edward Lewis (Richard Gere), who will help her reach her "immediate" money goal.

5. **What is the ticking clock?**

   Vivian's rent is due now and the landlord is throwing people out who are behind.

6. **What is the overall (to the end) External Story Goal planned for this character that you, as the author, know even if your character may be unaware of it?**

   Vivian's immediate external goal is to find security, but her External Story Goal (the one the author planned for her) is to change how she lives and works, so that she can find a better life.

7. How will this character's External Story Goal impact this his or her Internal Character Growth by the end of your story or how will this character's Internal Character Growth impact his or her External Story Goal?

When she finds a sense of security through the amount of money Edward pays her, Vivian gains confidence in herself and begins to see herself through his eyes, which will change how she perceives herself and her future.

8. Who are the key people present in this character's Everyday World?

Vivian's roommate.

9. What other significant characters will be in your story?

The hotel manager. Edward's lawyer. The grandfatherly shipping company owner.

10. Describe (show) three details (internal or external) about this character that will change over the course of the story.

Vivian pins her boots together, showing how flimsy and insecure her lifestyle is. She hides her hair, and her true persona, beneath a fake wig. She puts on a show of bravado to hide her true feelings.

Edward's Everyday World is living among superficial people and working on the next big business deal.

1. **When your story opens, what is this character doing and why?**

   Edward's at a party with lots of people, but very much alone. His latest girlfriend has broken up with him, because he keeps people at a great emotional distance.

2. **What is this character's expectation of what the future will bring?**

   Edward expects his future to be no different: bigger and better high-stake deals and he'll find another woman who'll appreciate his money.

3. **What is this character feeling internally (emotionally)?**

   Distant, empty, lonely, even if it's unknown to him.

4. **What event or action is about to happen to this character externally that will start the character toward his or her External Story Goal?**

   Most immediately, Edward is about to let Vivian (Julia Roberts), a hooker he meets when he asks for directions, drive his attorney's expensive manual-shift car back to the hotel. He invites her up for the night; then he decides to make her an offer to stay with him for a week.

5. **What is the ticking clock?**

   Edward must return to his home and business in New York at the end of the week.

6. **What is the overall (to the end) External Story Goal planned for this character that you as the author know, even if your character may be unaware of it?**

   His external goal that he is aware of is to acquire a family-owned business so he can dismantle it, but the author's External Story Goal for Edward is for him to change the way he does business by becoming partners with the owner of the business he originally wanted to take over.

7. **How will this character's External Story Goal impact this his or her Internal Character Growth by the end of your story or how will this character's Internal Character Growth impact his or her External Story Goal?**

   Because of associating with Vivian, Edward begins to change on a personal level to care about Vivian's feelings and how he treats her (his Internal Character Growth). By the time he has to make the final deal, Edward no longer wants to dismantle his adversary's company, but to become a partner.

8. **Who are the key people present in this character's Everyday World?**

   Edward's attorney.

9. **What other significant characters will be in your story?**

   Vivian; the older man who owns the business Edward wants to buy.

10. **Describe (show) three details (internal or external) about this character that will change over the course of the story.**

    Edward inhabits the penthouse suite alone. He is totally focused on business. He assumes money will buy everything he needs and accepts the limitations that assumption puts on his relationships.

EVERYDAY WORLD MOVIE EXAMPLE:
Casablanca

THE CHARACTER FOR THIS TEMPLATE IS:
Richard "Rick" Blaine (Humphrey Bogart)

Rick's Everyday World is running a bar in Casablanca during World War II, where black-market deals to gain exit visas are made in every dark corner.

1. **When your story opens, what is this character doing and why?**

   Rick owns a bar in Casablanca, ignoring the world at war and avoiding anyone who tries to engage him personally (he's neutral), because he keeps a wide distance from everyone, not getting personally involved in any way.

2. **What is this character's expectation of what the future will bring?**

   Rick knows the encroaching Nazi threat might alter Casablanca and the Vichy reign, but he believes this conflict does not have to impact him.

3. **What is this character feeling internally (emotionally)?**

   Rick gives the appearance of not caring if the Germans take control or not. His approach is to be apolitical and resolutely neutral.

4. **What event or action is about to happen to this character externally that will start the character toward his or her External Story Goal?**

   Rick is about to receive stolen transit papers to hold for a black-market dealer. He will find out the only woman he ever loved—Ilsa—is in Casablanca with a political refugee husband who cannot leave without transit papers.

5. **What is the ticking clock?**

   Ilsa's time is limited in Casablanca; either she finds a way to escape to Lisbon or she will be arrested by the Germans.

6. **What is the overall (to the end) External Story Goal planned for this character that you as the author know, even if your character may be unaware of it?**

   Rick's immediate external goal is to remain neutral, but his overall External Story Goal is to take a side in the German vs. anti-German political climate by aiding Ilsa and Laszlo in their escape.

7. **How will this character's External Story Goal impact this his or her Internal Character Growth by the end of your story or how will this character's Internal Character Growth impact his or her External Story Goal?**

   Ilsa's arrival and need to escape forces Rick to deal with the pain he's kept buried since she broke his heart in Paris. She makes him face how isolated and emotionally frozen he's been since then. She forces him to get involved and choose a side in the war.

8. **Who are the key people present in this character's Everyday World?**

   Sam, his piano player. The French Captain Renault. Rick's staff.

9. **What other significant characters will be in your story?**

   Ilsa (Rick's former lover), Victor Laszlo (her husband, a leader in the Resistance Movement), and the German major in Casablanca who wants to stop Laszlo.

10. **Describe (show) three details (internal or external) about this character that will change over the course of the story.**

    Rick will not drink nor socialize with any of his clients. He doesn't take political sides. He refuses to get involved in anyone else's problems.

This movie has a prologue, which means chapter one starts when Nemo wakes his father, Marlin, to take him to school. For this purpose, Marlin's Everyday World is the confines of his anemone home.

1. **When your story opens, what is this character doing and why?**

   Marlin is asleep, so Nemo is excitedly waking him up to have Marlin take him to his first day of school.

2. **What is this character's expectation of what the future will bring?**

   Marlin believes the world is dangerous and if he doesn't keep Nemo close to him, his only child could get hurt.

3. **What is this character feeling internally (emotionally)?**

   Marlin is feeling insecure, anxious, and untrusting.

4. **What event or action is about to happen to this character externally that will start the character toward his or her External Story Goal?**

   Marlin's only child is going to venture out of his "safe zone" and he will be captured by fish collectors.

5. **What is the ticking clock?**

   Marlin is convinced that to save Nemo, he must find Nemo immediately.

6. **What is the overall (to the end) planned for this character that you as the author know, even if your character may be unaware of it?**

   Marlin's immediate external goal and overall External Story Goal is to find and save his son.

7. How will this character's External Story Goal impact this his or her Internal Character Growth by the end of your story or how will this character's Internal Character Growth impact his or her External Story Goal?

   Searching for Nemo will force Marlin to face his greatest fear: that he might be a failure as a father, unable to protect his family. He'll learn that taking risks sometimes is part of life.

8. Who are the key people present in this character's Everyday World?

   Only Marlin's son Nemo.

9. What other significant characters will be in your story?

   Dory. The friendly sharks. Other neighbors.

10. Describe (show) three details (internal or external) about this character that will change over the course of the story.

    Marlin's inability to tell a good joke or story. Marlin's overprotectiveness and overreaction to a perceived hurt to Nemo. Marlin's inability to connect with others out of fear over the imagined threat to his family.

5 POWER PLOTTING
Premise Stated

> "A clear understanding of premise lays the groundwork for a great story."
> —Helen Scott Taylor, author of *The Magic Knot*

Premise often is used in conjunction with the word *theme*, both meaning something that's been laid out in advance to clue you into a behavior or an action that can happen in the future. It's the underlying meaning and essence of your story that many times can be reduced to a key word or phrase, oftentimes driving your protagonist.

Think in terms of a single idea, ideal, or quality such as family, connection, belief, revenge, trust, or even an expanded concept such as "to love you must first learn to trust," "no rich man enters the kingdom of heaven," or "truth wins out." The importance of premise or theme to your story (which many times is not obvious to you, the author, until you finish writing your rough draft) is that by understanding and honing your theme you can review everything from your character's actions and choices made to make sure you are showing your reader a consistent theme and are not leapfrogging around different concepts.

For example, you could start your story with the theme "trust before love," but halfway through your book you realize your protagonist does trust but doesn't believe that love is for them. So you continue to write with this new theme until the climax when the theme shifts one more time and becomes "truth will always triumph." The last quarter of your book carries this theme until the last scene in your story, when it once again becomes clear that "trust before love" is actually the lesson learned by your protagonist. Determining this theme means you can revise your story and strengthen it immeasurably by making sure the theme is clear throughout the story. Each stage gives the character a different example or lesson in how to learn their theme.

Theme is often uncovered by looking at your protagonist's Internal Character Growth: necessary for your protagonist or protagonists, but not for secondary characters. The Internal Character Growth is not something known from the character's POV, but an internal growth or change you, as the author, want this character to experience. It is this very change that sets commercial fiction apart from literary fiction.

In literary fiction, the protagonist is not expected to grow and change so much as to delve deeper into understanding the human condition. Commercial fiction readers want to see change over the course of a story. Therefore, the protagonist cannot simply attain an external goal (find the killer, save the planet, stop the land development), but must achieve an internal change or character growth (learn to love, learn to forgive, accept connection to others).

Some times your protagonist is not aware of a need to change internally. Think of Scarlett O'Hara in *Gone with the Wind* or Frodo Baggins in *Lord of the Rings*; both were quite content as they were and where they were. Their Everyday Worlds were perfect from *their* viewpoints, even as the Seeds of Change (which will be explained in Chapter 6) were pushing at them from outside their Everyday World.

The need to have internal change can be very unsettling and disruptive to your protagonist. In the movie *An Officer and a Gentleman*, Zack Mayo (Richard Gere) forced change on himself by signing up for officer cadet school. Zack did not think he had to make any internal changes, but he did have a clear External Story Goal to graduate from the course.

Some growth is forced on a character by the inciting incident in a story. In the movie *Gladiator*, General Maximus Decimus Meridius

(Russell Crowe) is thrust into a role of avenging murder and trying to save Rome after his family is slaughtered and he's forced to be a gladiator. At other times, the first steps toward the External Story Goal, which will lead to Internal Character Growth, are welcomed in part because the protagonist does not realize that the external events will create internal change.

> *Great characters know what they want.*
>
> —C. J. Box, *New York Times* best-selling author of *Blue Heaven*

Examples include the character of Charlie Babbitt (Tom Cruise) in *Rain Man* who is willing to take care of his autistic brother because he thinks the brother will make him rich. Charlie does not realize the internal change that will happen to him while getting to know his brother. In the movie *G.I. Jane*, Jordan O'Neill (Demi Moore) welcomes the chance to train as a Navy SEAL combat warrior. What she doesn't realize is how she'll internally change and grow in order to complete the training.

You, as the author, need to keep in mind the Internal Character Growth you are directing your protagonist toward so that the external events in the story create the change desired. Your protagonist might see only as far as the next scene goal, but you, as the story creator, should have a larger picture view of what is happening in your story.

The intention of this template is to move your character from their Everyday World to start on a path of change and growth. Keep in mind the character themselves may not want internal character growth or know how much change they will be experiencing as a result of taking an external action. This is a key transition phase of your story that will show your readers not only the motivation propelling your character to make change (both externally and internally), but also if the character is aware of this need for change and whether or not they welcome the External Story Goal. Or you can allow your character to think they are only taking a small step, when the reader is much more aware that this small step will have larger ramifications.

PREMISE STATED

The purpose for this template is to ensure the character will make significant internal change as he or she moves from their Everyday World, thus resulting in Internal Character Growth.

The Character for this template is:

----

1. What is this character's overall External Story Goal even if he or she is not yet aware of it (reference Question 6 answer in Chapter 4)?

----

2. What is this character lacking internally, i.e., security, connection, trust, hope, etc.?

----

3. What is this character's belief system? (If X happens, then Y will happen.)

----

4. How will this character's belief system change over the course of the story?

----

5. What is this character most afraid of internally and why?

----

6. When this character achieves his or her External Story Goal (question 1 above), will he or she also achieve what is missing internally (question 2 above) for this character? Why or why not?

----

7. What is the first significant decision/choice this character is given at the beginning of the story that will turn out nothing like he or she expects?

----

8. How does this character initially feel about this decision/choice?

> **TIP:** This is your character's normal internal reaction based on life up until the opening of your story.

----

9. How is this character going to eventually feel about this decision/choice?

> **TIP:** This is your character's internal reaction based on the changes that will have happened by the end of the story; this is the Internal Character Growth.

> **NOTE:** The character's "original" external goal—if he or she has one—at the beginning of the story is not always reached, but the External Story Goal you, as the author, plan for this character is reached. Also, the character must reach some form of Internal Character Growth.

POWER PLOTTING TIP

Your story premise is the basis of your story. The premise for *Cinderella* is "goodness will always triumph over adversity." The premise for *A Christmas Carol* is "greed will destroy you." The story arc encompasses your entire story from beginning to end with all the changes that occur in between. The idea is that there must be change; the end should be significantly different from the beginning and must show the purpose of the story. For instance: The story arc for *Cinderella* shows her starting in her Everyday World mopping floors as a maid in her own home, then getting a chance to go to a ball where she loses her slipper. The prince then hunts frantically for her; by the end of the movie *Cinderella* has met and fallen in love with the prince who loves her as well, then they marry and live happily ever after.

Premise: This is the story of one man's struggle with amnesia as he discovers his true identity as a trained CIA assassin.

1. **What is this character's overall External Story Goal even if he or she is not yet aware of it?**

    To stop Treadstone, even though Jason does not know they exist yet.

2. **What is this character lacking internally, i.e., security, connection, trust, hope, etc.?**

    Jason lacks the belief that he is a decent and good human being.

3. **What is this character's belief system? (If X happens, then Y will happen.)**

    If Jason discovers who he is, then his world will once again make sense.

4. **How will this character's belief system change over the course of the story?**

    Jason will discover that while he still won't have any memory of his past, he'll accept that he's a good man inside and not doomed to live the life he had in past.

5. **What is this character most afraid of internally and why?**

    Jason is afraid he will never discover his true identity and even if he does find out who he is, that he'll discover that he's a monster who kills.

6. **When this character achieves his or her External Story Goal (question 1 above) will he or she also achieve what is missing internally (question 2 above) for this character? Why or why not?**

    Yes, because by stopping Treadstone Jason realizes that he is a decent and good human being.

7. What is the first significant decision/choice this character is given at the beginning of the story that will turn out nothing like he or she expects?

    Jason goes to Zurich thinking the contents of the safe-deposit box will tell him who he is, but there are so many documents identifying him by different names it only creates more questions.

8. How does this character initially feel about this decision/choice?

    Jason has no choice since this is his only lead, so he feels encouraged and anxious.

9. How is this character going to eventually feel about this decision/choice?

    Although it's disappointing at first, he will eventually be glad that this led him to meet Marie.

Premise: A Cinderella story of a prostitute who meets and falls in love with an emotionally void business magnate who learns to love because of her and marries her.

1. **What is this character's overall External Story Goal even if he or she is not yet aware of it?**

   Vivian's goal is to leave prostitution and find a better life.

2. **What is this character lacking internally, i.e., security, connection, trust, hope, etc.?**

   Vivian lacks the ability to believe in herself, that she is more than simply a hooker, or that she can change her life.

3. **What is this character's belief system? (If X happens, then Y will happen.)**

   That if Vivian falls emotionally for a man, then she ends up out on the street, so she might as well keep her heart out of the picture with men and use them the way they use her.

4. **How will this character's belief system change over the course of the story?**

   She will learn that she is more than her job. When she begins to perceive herself differently (i.e., with value), so will others, which will allow her to move beyond what she is today and toward a person to be respected.

5. **What is this character most afraid of internally and why?**

    Vivian is afraid that she really is nothing more than white trash and a hooker, because she got the message early in her life that she wouldn't amount to anything. When she tried to move beyond her childhood roots, life beat her down until the only option she saw open was to become what others treated her like anyway: a disposable encounter.

6. **When this character achieves his or her External Story Goal (question 1) will he or she also achieve what is missing internally (question 2) for this character? Why or why not?**

    Yes, because Vivian must reach the point that she believes in herself for her to use what she's gained (monetarily and materially) during the week with Edward to search for a better way of life and a better job.

7. **What is the first significant decision/choice this character is given at the beginning of the story that will turn out nothing like he or she expects?**

    Vivian accepts Edward's offer for her to earn a week's worth of wages—more money than she's ever had—for staying with him seven days.

8. **How does this character initially feel about this decision/choice?**

    Vivian is willing to do whatever is necessary to change herself externally to meet his expectations to earn that money.

9. **How is this character going to eventually feel about this decision/choice?**

    As Vivian works to adapt and fit into Edward's world, she'll begin to move away from her world and start to experience what it feels like to be a different person with a different future. This causes her to question what she's accepted as unchangeable, and ultimately she realizes she may have to lose Edward to gain herself.

Premise: Love conquers all.

1. **What is this character's overall External Story Goal even if he or she is not yet aware of it?**

   Edward's External Story Goal is to change the way he does business by becoming partners with the owner of the business he originally wanted to take over.

2. **What is this character lacking internally, i.e., security, connection, trust, hope, etc.?**

   Edward lacks the ability to connect or bond with another person or to be intimate, so he never has a true relationship with anyone in business or personally.

3. **What is this character's belief system? (If X happens, then Y will happen.)**

   If Edward allows anyone to get close to him, then they'll only disappoint and hurt him. Edward believes in his ability to do business without an emotional input, because he is not willing to trust a decision based on emotions.

4. **How will this character's belief system change over the course of the story?**

   Edward will learn to trust his gut feeling as much as what he knows externally about a situation. He'll learn that if he gets to know a woman or a business competitor well enough and allows them to know him, then he can trust his instincts when it comes to making a decision.

5. **What is this character most afraid of internally and why?**

   Trust. Edward trusted his father to love him and instead his father abandoned him. Edward fears that if he trusts his heart to another human being (not just a woman) again he will be abandoned and hurt.

6. When this character achieves his or her External Story Goal (question 1) will he or she also achieve what is missing internally (question 2) for this character? Why or why not?

Yes. By deciding to form a partnership with the shipping company owner, Edward is clearly willing to make a commitment to another person, which allows him to take the risk to offer Vivian a full relationship not based on a monetary agreement, but on a depth of emotion.

7. What is the first significant decision/choice this character is given at the beginning of the story that will turn out nothing like he or she expects?

Faced with a week alone since he now has no girlfriend, Edward decides to make Vivian—a hooker clearly motivated by money, which he understands—an offer to stay with him for a week to be his companion at social engagements.

8. How does this character initially feel about this decision/choice?

It's simply a business deal like any other negotiations Edward enters into to get what he wants and can control.

9. How is this character going to eventually feel about this decision/choice?

By inviting Vivian into his life, Edward comes to care for her and his ability to control his emotional reaction to people slips from his fingers. The stakes rise as he realizes it may take more than money to win Vivian's love.

Premise: This is the story of a man who is willing to sacrifice everything for the woman he loves, which includes walking away so that she will have a future. True love means sacrifice.

1. **What is this character's overall External Story Goal even if he or she is not yet aware of it?**

   For Rick to make a commitment to someone, take a side in the German conflict, and return to being a resistance fighter.

2. **What is this character lacking internally, i.e., security, connection, trust, hope, etc.?**

   Rick lacks connection; the ability to care what happens to another person or to the world around him or to interact with others on a personal level.

3. **What is this character's belief system? (If X happens, then Y will happen.)**

   Rick believes if he cares about anyone other than himself, then he will eventually end up alone and hurt. Therefore, it is better to not care and just be alone.

4. **How will this character's belief system change over the course of the story?**

   In the end, Rick believes he can make a difference and, in doing so, he'll regain a part of him that had died.

5. **What is this character most afraid of internally and why?**

   Rick's afraid of feeling again and the pain that comes with it.

6. When this character achieves his or her External Story Goal (question 1) will he or she also achieve what is missing internally (question 2) for this character? Why or why not?

   Yes, because by making a commitment to help Ilsa and Laszlo plus taking a side in the German conflict, Rick has reconnected with people and again cares about the world around him.

7. What is the first significant decision/choice this character is given at the beginning of the story that will turn out nothing like he expects?

   Rick becomes the possessor of two Letters of Transit, which means he can either destroy the papers (if he's really neutral) or give them to two people who will get safe passage out of Casablanca to Lisbon and thus to freedom and safety in America; he must choose to use them or not.

8. How does this character initially feel about this decision/choice?

   Rick thinks the papers are more an annoyance, since so many people want to get the letters from him, including the French police and the Germans.

9. How is this character going to eventually feel about this decision/choice?

   Rick realizes he holds the key to Ilsa's freedom and safety in his hands, which makes him realize he isn't the cold, heartless man he's pretended to be for so long when he decides to help her escape.

Premise: This is the story of a father changing from being an overprotective parent—who stifles his only child's existence—to embracing the world so they both have fuller lives. What does parental love mean?

1. **What is this character's overall External Story Goal even if he or she is not yet aware of it?**

   To find and save his son Nemo.

2. **What is this character lacking internally, i.e., security, connection, trust, hope, etc.?**

   Marlin has such a narrow definition of what a good father is—someone who will shield his son from any threat—that he doesn't let Nemo experience life. So he's lacking a broader definition of being a parent.

3. **What is this character's belief system? (If X happens, then Y will happen.)**

   If Marlin isn't constantly vigilant then something bad will happen to Nemo.

4. **How will this character's belief system change over the course of the story?**

   Marlin will learn that in trying to protect his son, Marlin was also keeping Nemo from enjoying the good parts of life.

5. **What is this character most afraid of internally and why?**

   Marlin is afraid if he's not with his son every minute, Nemo will get hurt and probably die.

6. **When this character achieves his or her External Story Goal (question 1) will he or she also achieve what is missing internally (question 2) for this character? Why or why not?**

   Yes, by saving Nemo, Marlin will have gained experience along the way that will have taught him a broader definition of being a parent.

7. What is the first significant decision/choice this character is given at the beginning of the story that will turn out nothing like he or she expects?

Marlin agrees to take Nemo to his first day of school.

8. How does this character initially feel about this decision/choice?

Marlin doesn't want Nemo to go to school yet and believes everything outside his home is a potential danger. He doesn't really know his neighbors and doesn't want to.

9. How is this character going to eventually feel about this decision/choice?

Marlin learns to build friendships (such as his friendship with Dory) and that not everyone is evil (like the shark going through a program to stop eating others), and that Nemo deserves to grow up experiencing life.

6 POWER PLOTTING
Seeds of Change—Pros and Cons

" Change isn't believable for a reader unless well
motivated. "

—Liz Jasper, author of *Underdead*

What's happened so far in your story?

You've established your primary character or characters, have shown their External Story Goal or maybe a character's Immediate External Goal (which is a first step toward a larger External Story Goal they may be unaware of as yet), given at least a glimpse of what internally may be either driving the primary character(s) toward the External Story Goal or the Immediate External Goal, or what is keeping them from rushing after the goal.

Now you're in a key section of your story that a lot of newer authors tend to either ignore or place in the wrong section of their novels. This next area of your story—Seeds of Change and Pros and Cons—serves a very important dramatic function. This is when you let your reader know several key pieces of information.

The first key piece is to let the reader know that whatever external event or task the character is about to embark on—whether it's to pull together a winning peewee softball team or climb an unassailable mountain or take an emotional risk with someone—it contains elements of risk for that character. This isn't necessarily a physical danger, but could be an emotional danger. The idea is that for the character to go after either their Immediate External Goal or overall External Story Goal will not be easy, and thus the struggle to reach that External Story Goal is worthy of having the reader continue with the story to the end to see if it is indeed reached.

In other words, make the goal matter to the character in order to make it matter to a reader.

This is the place in your story where you can weave in Back Story in small bits about your character. The Back Story should serve a purpose, such as giving an explanation of what made the character who they are. This is also the place to share the character's world view—love hurts, taking risks can backfire, it's easy to have one's reputation shredded. Many times these world views hold the seed of what is lacking in their Internal Character Growth. This world view often makes attaining their External Story Goal more of a challenge.

An example of this phase of Seeds of Change and Pros and Cons would be from the *Chronicles of Riddick*. After a dramatic action opening, Riddick (Vin Diesel) travels to another planet to see why a bounty was placed on him. Once he's on the planet, he's told the bounty was to draw him out *because* that planet and all its inhabitants need his help or they will be destroyed by the encroaching Necromongers. The Seeds of Change, or what is about to happen, are sown in Riddick when he is asked to help, but his response is "Not my fight." This is not hesitation; this is a flat out "no," which tells the viewer that Riddick has reasons not to help.

In the movie *G.I. Jane*, when Jordan (Demi Moore) is given the opportunity to join the training squad and try out for a coveted Navy SEAL position her response contains no hesitation—she's thrilled; this is a dream come true. Yet she does not rush off, but is shown in an intimate interlude with her boyfriend. The purpose of this scene is to clue the viewer in to the fact that if she does leave to be trained and then is deployed as a SEAL, her relationship with him is at risk. His role is to point out the cons of her leaving, which increases the story tension and lets the viewer know that even change that is welcomed contains risk.

The same is the case with the romantic comedy *Notting Hill*. The Seeds of Change occur when William Thacker (Hugh Grant) brings Anna Scott (Julia Roberts) into his house to clean her up after he spilled juice all over her. This scene shows that there could be a relationship between the two of them if they both got out of their own way. The Pros and Cons happen after William lets Anna leave. He later discusses with other characters how knowing a relationship with her would never happen for a guy like him. The viewer gets to see that both characters are averse to taking a risk in the relationship department.

> *My creative muse might be struggling on what to write next, but if I read my plot notes, I can begin writing a previously planned scene until I get my groove back.*
>
> —Kelly Parra, RITA award finalist for her debut Young Adult book *Graffiti Girl*

The intention of this template is to thread in the character's Immediate External Goal that will eventually lead the character to his or her External Story Goal. At the same time, you, as the author, will show a reader the reasons this particular character holds a belief system or world view that is keeping him or her from being a whole and well-rounded individual. This information alerts the reader to the Internal Character Growth the character must struggle toward or acts as a reference point of change along the way that will show that Internal Character Growth has happened by the end of the story.

SEEDS OF CHANGE—PROS AND CONS

The purpose of this template is to ensure that change is actually happening and the character is not just going from one event or action to the next. It must be clear there is a cost or consequence to the character whether they take action or not.

The Character for this template is:

---

1. What external action or event is happening as a result of the decision (reference question 7 answer in Chapter 5) this character has made that's about to change his or her life?

---

2. What internal conflict does this action (reference question 1 above) create in this character's life?

   PLOT HOLE ALERT: If this action does not create an internal conflict, then create an additional strong external conflict.

   TIP ON QUESTIONS 3–7: These are possible outcomes to explore for your character.

3. What could happen if this character *doesn't* achieve or reach his or her External Story Goal? (This should have significant repercussions for the character.)

---

4. What will happen if this character *does* achieve or reach his or her External Story Goal?

----

5. What could happen if this character *doesn't* achieve or reach his or her Internal Character Growth?

----

6. What will happen if this character *does* achieve or reach his or her Internal Character Growth, and thus changes internally by the end of the story?

----

7. What is it about this character's personality/belief that is an obstacle to his or her Internal Character Growth?

----

8. Who else will be impacted personally—and in what way—by the changes about to happen (as referenced in question 1)?

----

9. What decision/choice does this character make next that will force an action to be taken?

TIP: This action will change the course of the story, and should happen about a quarter to a third of the way through your story.

---------------------------------   ---

---------   --

----

10. What action is taken as a result of question 9?

-----------------------------   --

---   ---------------------------------

POWER PLOTTING TIP A Plot Hole is an area of your story that may not be working as hard as it could to advance character growth, increase risks, or show change. In the strongest plots, no scene can be removed without impacting the primary story line. A Plot Hole can allow the reader to set the book down and walk away. A Plot Hole also means your story is lagging, that action is happening that does not move the story forward as strongly as it could be moved. The hole creates wasted words. An example is a fast-paced story where the characters stop to eat a meal in a restaurant. If that meal is necessary to the story, to give the characters time to reveal key information or to show character development or to strengthen a relationship or, best of all, all three, then the restaurant scene belongs. (See the movie *The Bourne Identity* for an example of a restaurant scene that does all three.) But, if the scene is there to show the restaurant to add color to the story or because one of the characters likes this restaurant, then you have a potential plot hole.

For Jason Bourne, every step closer to discovering who he is makes him realize he might not want the answers he's discovering.

1. **What external action or event is happening as a result of the decision (reference question 7 answer in Chapter 5) this character has made that's about to change his or her life?**

   When Jason and Marie reach his flat in Paris, he encounters an assassin and realizes he is a man wanted by an unknown enemy, but he can't leave Marie (she's in shock) even though he needs to run alone.

2. **What internal conflict does this action (reference question 1 above) create in this character's life?**

   As a result of his not being able to abandon Marie, Jason realizes they are both in danger and he is not free to run and hide, which shows he is a good man even though he doesn't consciously realize it.

3. **What could happen if this character *doesn't* achieve or reach his or her External Story Goal?**

   If Jason doesn't find out why someone wants him dead, he will have to run indefinitely until he's killed.

4. **What will happen if this character *does* achieve or reach his or her External Story Goal?**

   Learning his true identity means Jason will have to face that he might not like what he discovers about himself or what he's done in his past.

5. **What could happen if this character *doesn't* achieve or reach his or her Internal Character Growth?)**

   Jason will never have a chance at a normal life or a relationship with a woman like Marie.

6. What will happen if this character *does* achieve or reach his or her Internal Character Growth, and thus changes internally by the end of the story?

   Jason will have to face his past and reconcile who he once was with who he is today.

7. What is it about this character's personality/belief that is an obstacle to his or her Internal Character Growth?

   Jason's belief is that if in the past you did bad things then you must be a bad person. This is an obstacle because it prevents him from believing he is a good man.

8. Who else will be impacted personally—and in what way—by the changes about to happen (as referenced in question 1)?

   Marie, because she believes he's a better person than he thinks he is, and as a result, her decision to remain with Jason puts her life in danger, too.

9. What decision/choice does this character make that will force an action to be taken?

   Jason chooses to start looking more actively into his past when he gains a clue about having been at a Paris hotel.

10. What action is taken as a result of question 9?

    At Marie's encouragement, Jason follows a trail of phone calls from his previous hotel stay under an alias, which lead him to a shipping group that he can tie to an African dictator who is then murdered.

SEEDS OF CHANGE—PROS AND CONS MOVIE EXAMPLE:
Pretty Woman

THE CHARACTER FOR THIS TEMPLATE IS:
Vivian Ward (Julia Roberts)

Vivian Ward is about to discover that to fit into Edward's high-class and high-powered world will mean more than a change of clothes, it'll mean a change of mind-set.

1. **What external action or event is happening as a result of the decision (reference question 7 answer in Chapter 5) this character has made that's about to change his or her life?**

   Upon agreeing to stay with Edward for the upcoming week, she must now learn to fit into his world by buying an appropriate wardrobe.

2. **What internal conflict does this action (reference question 1 above) create in this character's life?**

   Seeing herself as reflected in Edward's eyes and through the eyes of people who don't treat her like a hooker, Vivian begins to experience what her life would be like if she was not a prostitute and yearns to be that woman for real.

3. **What could happen if this character *doesn't* achieve or reach his or her External Story Goal?**

   Vivian will return to the streets and her old way of life, never finding the security or the respect she's enjoyed briefly.

4. **What will happen if this character *does* achieve or reach his or her External Story Goal?**

   As others start accepting Vivian as having value, including Edward, they will have expectations of her as a person that will prevent her from continuing with a life as a prostitute.

5. **What could happen if this character** *doesn't* **achieve or reach his or her Internal Character Growth?)**

   Vivian will never again experience life as a respected woman and have the freedom to choose a man with whom she can have a true relationship.

0. **What will happen if this character** *does* **achieve or reach his or her Internal Character Growth, and thus changes internally by the end of the story?**

   Vivian will rise to her own secret expectations for herself. She'll become the woman she always envisioned who deserves to have a champion in shining armor love her.

7. **What is it about this character's personality/belief that is an obstacle to his or her Internal Character Growth?**

   Deep inside, Vivian questions if she is worthy of being someone valued and loved.

8. **Who else will be impacted personally—and in what way—by the changes about to happen (as referenced in question 1)?**

   Edward, because once he perceives Vivian differently, he starts treating her differently and reacting to her differently than he ever has to other women in the past, which causes him to have a harder time keeping their relationship strictly business. Vivian's roommate, because as Vivian morphs into a different woman, it influences her roommate's ability to change as well.

9. **What decision does this character make that will force an action to be taken?**

   Vivian is unable to purchase a dress for dinner with Edward that evening because the snooty Rodeo Drive sales clerks treat her as they see her—like a streetwalker who belongs on the street. Vivian first accepts their judgment of her and walks away Then she meets the hotel manager and decides to trust him with her dilemma.

10. **What action is taken as a result of question 9?**

    The hotel manager befriends Vivian, who desperately needs and wants a friend. Then he hooks Vivian up with someone who helps her pick a dress.

Edward Lewis thinks he's bought a hooker for a week-long companion, but he's about to discover he's acquired a whole lot more.

1. **What external action or event is happening as a result of the decision (reference question 7 answer in Chapter 5) this character has made that's about to change his or her life?**

    Edward needs a date for dinner that night with the owner of the company he's about to acquire, so he sends Vivian out to get a dress.

2. **What internal conflict does this action (reference question 1 above) create in this character's life?**

    When Edward sees her in her new clothes, he starts to view Vivian with new eyes. He feels enchanted by the way others accept her at first glance and how she connects easily with others, which he can't. Because of Vivian's interaction with the grandfatherly businessman, Edward also finds that he likes the man even though Edward never allows emotions to enter into a business decision.

3. **What could happen if this character *doesn't* achieve or reach his or her External Story Goal?**

    Edward will continue to be alone, surrounded by superficial people and he will continue to dismantle companies and destroy the lives of others.

4. **What will happen if this character *does* achieve or reach his or her External Story Goal?**

    Edward could begin to build things: ships, as well as business and personal relationships.

5. **What could happen if this character *doesn't* achieve or reach his or her Internal Character Growth?**

   Edward will continue on a path of becoming his father—cold, isolated and hated—and die a lonely old man estranged from everyone.

6. **What will happen if this character *does* achieve or reach his or her Internal Character Growth, and thus changes internally by the end of the story?**

   Edward risks being hurt again as he was when his father turned his back on him as a young boy, but he also faces the potential of a life with someone who will love him in return.

7. **What is it about this character's personality/beliefs that is an obstacle to his or her Internal Character Growth?**

   Having been abandoned as a child, Edward can't see past his anger with his father to trust another person.

8. **Who else will be impacted personally—and in what way—by the changes about to happen (as referenced in question 1)?**

   Vivian, because as she pushes Edward to change and to be the better man she sees inside him, she begins to see the better woman she can be who deserves honest love. Edward's lawyer; when Edward starts to transform, it alters the way he does business. The lawyer is frightened of losing the obscene amount of money he makes on Edward's corporate raiding.

9. **What decision/choice does this character make next that will force an action to be taken?**

   Upon Vivian pointing out after the business dinner that the grandfatherly businessman and his grandson are nice people, Edward realizes he was beginning to think so as well. He decides he's lowered his guard and almost allowed emotions to enter his business decisions.

10. **What action is taken as a result of question 9?**

    In response to Vivian's comments, he retreats physically and emotionally from Vivian when they return to his penthouse. He goes downstairs to play the piano for strangers.

Rick Blaine's past is about to collide with his present and force choices that could negatively impact the future of many, including Rick.

1. **What external action or event is happening as a result of the decision (reference question 7 answer in Chapter 5) this character has made that's about to change his or her life?**

   Now that Rick has the stolen documents, he is on the German major's radar and Ilsa, plus her husband, re-enters his life with a need for two Letters of Transit.

2. **What internal conflict does this action (reference question 1 above) create in this character's life?**

   Rick will have to face his pain and grief over abandonment to help Ilsa, which means learning the truth about why she did not meet him at the train station and facing why he stopped fighting for freedom.

3. **What could happen if this character *doesn't* achieve or reach his or her External Story Goal?**

   Ilsa and her husband stand to be put in a concentration camp or killed.

4. **What will happen if this character *does* achieve or reach his or her External Story Goal?**

   Rick himself stands to be arrested and put in a concentration camp or killed for aiding Laszlo.

5. **What could happen if this character *doesn't* achieve or reach his or her Internal Character Growth?**

   Rick will continue to remain bitter and alone, emotionally broken.

6. **What will happen if this character *does* achieve or reach his or her Internal Character Growth, and thus changes internally by the end of the story?**

   Rick will open himself back up to caring again. Caring could bring more emotional pain, but it will also make him feel whole again.

7. **What is it about this character's personality/belief that is an obstacle to his or her Internal Character Growth?**

   Having been hurt and disillusioned before, Rick is reluctant to care again or get involved personally.

8. **Who else will be impacted personally—and in what way—by the changes about to happen (as referenced in question 1)?**

   Ilsa will have to make a choice between the two men—Rick and her husband—she loves in different ways. Victor Laszlo learns his wife loved another man and must face giving her up to save her. The French Captain Renault stands to lose his position and possibly his life by getting involved in Laszlo's escape and the murder of a German major.

9. **What decision/choice does this character make next that will force an action to be taken?**

   Rick decides to sit with Renault, Ilsa, and Laszlo (her husband) to have drinks.

10. **What action is taken as a result of question 9?**

   Renault points out how out of character this is for Rick and begins to ask him questions about his feelings toward Ilsa.

For Marlin, taking his son, Nemo, to school is fraught with danger and this first step leads to even greater dangers.

1. What external action or event is happening as a result of the decision (reference question 7 answer in Chapter 5) this character has made that's about to change his or her life?

   Marlin's only child is about to be taken by a fish collector.

2. What internal conflict does this action (reference question 1 above) create in this character's life?

   When the fish collector takes Nemo, in order to save his son's life, Marlin will have to overcome his fear of danger in the larger ocean.

3. What could happen if this character *doesn't* achieve or reach his or her External Story Goal?

   If Marlin does not find and save Nemo, his son will be lost forever.

4. What will happen if this character *does* achieve or reach his or her External Story Goal?

   Marlin will save Nemo's life plus discover ways to help Nemo and himself live more fully in the bigger world.

5. What could happen if this character *doesn't* achieve or reach his or her Internal Character Growth?

   Marlin will continue to stunt Nemo's life and lose his son emotionally, which will make Marlin feel like a failure as a father.

6. **What will happen if this character *does* achieve or reach his or her Internal Character Growth, and thus changes internally by the end of the story?**

Then Marlin will have to accept that he can't protect Nemo forever. He will discover that teaching his child independence is a sacrifice all parents must make in their child's best interest.

7. **What is it about this character's personality/belief that is an obstacle to his or her Internal Character Growth?**

Marlin is so terrified that he can't keep Nemo safe that he is unwilling to risk letting his only child experience life.

8. **Who else will be impacted personally—and in what way—by the changes about to happen (as referenced in question 1)?**

Nemo, because his life will open up. Dory, who will become Marlin's friend, and will be accepted into his community of fish. Marlin's neighbors, who will be given a chance to know Marlin as he joins the community more.

9. **What decision/choice does this character make next that will force an action to be taken?**

Marlin decides to go after Nemo.

10. **What action is taken as a result of question 9?**

Marlin ventures out from his safe haven into unknown and dangerous waters and meets Dory.

7 POWER PLOTTING
Momentum—Decision—Push

> "One-half of knowing what you want is knowing what you must give up before you get it."
> —Sidney Howard, screenwriter of *Gone with the Wind*

You've left your character hesitating to take action because you've spelled out the risk, the potential problems, and all the smart reasons not to act. So how do you move them forward to act? You create plausible motivation and involve a mentor (this character might already be introduced, but not deeply involved yet) who provides the incentive to take action instead of allowing the character to continue to weigh the Pros and Cons. The role of a mentor is twofold:

1. To give gifts that could help the protagonist as the story unfolds. The gifts can be tangible—a key, a map, a magic wand; or intangible—advice, guidance, lessons.
2. The gift and the mentor both create the second key element: to get the story moving.

This phase can be rich with conflict and emotion and gives the author more opportunity to clarify what's at stake for the protagonist or character if action is or isn't taken. Mentors are not always welcomed by the protagonist: for example, when a mentor uses shame or derision to provoke action, or issues a warning that's ignored. The reader can often see the mentor's function more clearly than the character can.

Keep in mind the mentor does not need to be a person but could be a code—or a belief system. It could be a voice from the past or a creed drummed into someone since childhood. The mentor can also be directing the protagonist to some action that is not for the protagonist's own good. Think of the *Alias* TV series where the protagonist Sydney Bristow (Jennifer Garner) was tricked by a family friend and father figure into working for the bad guys. Nikita (Peta Wilson) in the TV series *La Femme Nikita* was in constant conflict with her mentor—Michael—during the early seasons by not quite trusting if he was with her or against her. In romantic fiction, the hero or heroine often can act as mentor to the other at this and other phases in the story.

> *Great pacing is narrative so compelling that your reader races across every word and doesn't skip a thing.*
>
> —Mario Acevedo, best-selling author of the Felix Gomez vampire-detective series

Other examples of mentors include the geeky roommate in *Notting Hill* who, at key story changes, encourages William Thacker (Hugh Grant) to go after the girl of his dreams. In *Bridget Jones's Diary*, her circle of friends acts as the mentor to Bridget. In many buddy movies, it's the buddy who acts as mentor to the protagonist—think Martin Riggs (Mel Gibson) and Roger Murtaugh (Danny Glover) in the *Lethal Weapon* movie series and Mike Lowrey (Will Smith) and Marcus Burnett (Martin Lawrence) in *Bad Boys*. In *Men in Black*, Agent K (Tommy Lee Jones) is the mentor to Agent J (Will Smith) until Agent J becomes the mentor to his new partner at the end of the first movie.

The function of this template is to introduce a mentor into your story who acts as the catalyst and motivates the protagonist to act and move the story forward in spite of all the good reasons just given to not act. This template brings the character's need for Internal Character Growth and External Story Goal or the character's Immediate External Goal together, creating clear motivation for the next story phase where an Action Taken will change the story.

MOMENTUM—DECISION—PUSH

The purpose for this template is to give the character a clear motivation for moving forward to take an action the character does not want to take. (Tip: This is almost a quarter to a third of the way into your story.)

The Character for this template is:

TIP: The character for this template is not the mentor, but a primary character.

1. Who is giving advice to this character at this point?

    TIP: This is an advisory character who will help or force the primary character to take action that he or she may not otherwise want to take. This advisory character is also known as a mentor who allows the reader to see hat even though action is difficult for the primary character, he or she is given strong enough motivation to act anyway. Note: A mentor is a "catalyst" as well as a guide or advisor, and there may be more than one mentor at times.

    ----

2. Are any gifts given by the mentor, which will make the decision to act easier for this character? If so, what are these gifts?

    TIP: Gifts can be tangible such as a map, key, codeword, etc.; or intangible such as a belief, understanding, emotional support, insights, etc.

    ----

3. What decision does this character now make?

    ----

4. How does this character feel about the decision?

----

5. What action does this character take next?

----

6. Is there a person who initially attempts to block this character from making a change or reaching his or her external goal and, if so, how?

   TIP: This is a Threshold Guardian.

POWER PLOTTING TIP The mentor is a character who advises or aids the primary character to finally make a decision and act. This is an archetypal role out of Jungian psychology and is sometimes called the Wise Old Man or Wise Old Woman. A Threshold Guardian is someone who (temporarily) blocks your main character from reaching his or her goal. This sets up a test for your character to prove how important the goal is. If a Threshold Guardian can stop a character completely from moving forward, then the character is not sufficiently motivated to reach that goal.

1. **Who is giving advice to this character at this point?**

   Marie is encouraging Jason to search for answers.

2. **Are any gifts given by the mentor, which will make the decision to act easier for this character? If so what are these gifts?**

   Though it's obvious, even with amnesia, that Jason is a man who can take care of himself, it is Marie who forces him beyond his hesitation to discover more about his past. When she bluntly tells Jason to figure out his past, this gives him the push necessary to discover his past to allow for the possibility of a different future. Plus, she physically steps in to help by going into the hotel to retrieve documents he needs.

3. **What decision does this character now make?**

   Jason decides to call all the numbers referenced on the document from the hotel where he'd been listed under an alias.

4. **How does this character feel about this decision?**

   Jason is wary about what he might discover, but determined to move forward.

5. **What action does this character take next?**

   Jason gets a lead on a ship company that knew him by the alias Jason Bourne. He visits the company where he finds information related to an African leader.

6. **Is there a person who initially attempts to block this character from making a change or reaching his or her external goal and, if so, how?**

   The CIA handler is the Threshold Guardian, because he attempts to block Jason from change. The handler is trying to get Jason to return to the CIA to bring him back into the fold.

Pretty Woman

THE CHARACTER FOR THIS TEMPLATE IS:
Vivian Ward (Julie Roberts)

1. **Who is giving advice to this character at this point?**
   The hotel manager.

2. **Are any gifts given by the mentor, which will make the decision to act easier for this character? If so, what are these gifts?**
   By making arrangements to have Vivian dressed by the hotel boutique clerk, the hotel manager gives her an alternative to working with the snooty shop clerks on Rodeo Drive who would not sell her clothes. Because he treats Vivian with respect, she starts to feel differently about herself. All of this allows Vivian entry to Edward's world as she joins him for a business dinner with the owners of the shipping business.

3. **What decision does this character now make?**
   Vivian decides to trust the hotel manager, whose advice results in her being transformed into a stunning yet respectable woman with the confidence to join Edward for the evening.

4. **How does this character feel about this decision?**
   Vivian is relieved that she can step into Edward's world as an equal to other women for that night.

5. **What action does this character take next?**
   Vivian attends the fancy dinner where Edward meets with the owner and grandson of the company Edward is trying to acquire.

6. **Is there a person who initially attempts to block this character from making a change or reaching his or her external goal and, if so, how?**
   The snooty shop saleswomen are Threshold Guardians, because they attempt to block Vivian from change. They attempted to keep Vivian from entering their Rodeo Drive world by denying her access to the proper clothes and reinforcing that she is no more than a common hooker.

1. **Who is giving advice to this character at this point?**

   Vivian, who points out to Edward that she likes the grandfatherly owner of the company Edward is trying to acquire, something Edward has ignored until now.

2. **Are any gifts given by the mentor, which will make the decision to act easier for this character? If so, what are these gifts?**

   Vivian gives Edward honest answers to questions, which force him to face the personal side of doing business when everyone else tells him what they think he wants to hear. She tells Edward he could change the way he does business, broaching a taboo subject that hits a nerve.

3. **What decision does this character now make?**

   Edward redoubles his efforts to take over the company, refusing to allow emotion to cloud his judgment.

4. **How does this character feel about this decision?**

   This is an emotional reaction to the realization that in another situation Edward would like to work with and learn from the grandfatherly man vs. destroying him. Edward is pulling back inside himself in reaction to almost letting down his emotional guard.

5. **What action does this character take next?**

   Because Edward will need Vivian to accompany him to more social events, he instructs her to buy more clothes. This is when he learns about Vivian being snubbed by the snooty shop girls and he takes her back to Rodeo Drive himself as her champion.

6. **Is there a person who initially attempts to block this character from making a change or reaching his or her external goal and, if so, how?**

   The grandfatherly businessman is a Threshold Guardian, because he is initially blocking Edward from reaching his goal by making Edward care what happens to a business that took forty years to build.

1. **Who is giving advice to this character at this point?**

   Renault points out to Rick how out of character it is for Rick to sit and visit with customers, cluing the viewer into the fact that a major change in Rick's behavior is already happening.

2. **Are any gifts given by the mentor, which will make the decision to act easier for this character? If so, what are these gifts?**

   Renault warns Rick about the missing Letters of Transit and not to get involved or try to help Laszlo.

3. **What decision does this character now make?**

   Rick decides to wait to see if Ilsa returns after hours.

4. **How does this character feel about this decision?**

   Rick is thrown off-guard by seeing Ilsa again, and his feelings of pain and abandonment resurface.

5. **What action does this character take next?**

   Rick refuses to listen to Ilsa's explanation when she arrives, shutting her down and driving her away.

6. **Is there a person who initially attempts to block this character from making a change or reaching his or her external goal and, if so, how?**

   Sam is the Threshold Guardian, because he tries to get Rick to avoid dealing with Ilsa and getting involved.

1. Who is giving advice to this character at this point?

   Note: As referenced in the template, a mentor can be a catalyst as well as a guide or advisor, and there may at times be more than one mentor, which is the case in this story. The dentist-diver (catalyst) forces Marlin into action and Dory leads Marlin through dangerous waters (guide).

2. Are any gifts given by the mentor, which will make the decision to act easier for this character? If so, what are these gifts?

   By kidnapping Nemo, the dentist-diver forces Marlin to expand his experience with the world and face his fears. By swimming along with Marlin, Dory helps hunt for Nemo, reassuring Marlin there is good in the larger world and not just frightening things.

3. What decision does this character now make?

   Marlin decides to swim after Nemo and go as far as he can go to find his son.

4. How does this character feel about this decision?

   Marlin is wary but determined.

5. What action does this character take next?

   Marlin swims with Dory until they encounter a shark.

6. Is there a person who initially attempts to block this character from making a change or reaching his or her external goal and, if so, how?

   The three sharks are Threshold Guardians, because they try to eat Marlin and, if the sharks succeed, then Marlin's External Story Goal—to find and save Nemo—will end.

According to Roget's Thesaurus, **twist** means "Rotate; revolve; spin; curve; turn."

8 POWER PLOTTING
Action Taken—Twist Point One

" We are men of action, lies do not become us. "
—William Goldman, author and screenwriter of
The Princess Bride and *Marathon Man*

You are now about a quarter to a third of the way into your novel. You've reached Twist Point One when, due to Action Taken, your protagonist will be changed forever. This does not have to be a huge change, but is a clue to the reader that an important threshold has been reached and passed, and must impact the character's gradual Internal Character Growth. Most people do not make a major internal change in one big leap or after just one test. Your character's concerns, hesitations, and reasons to either act or not act have been weighed (Chapter 6) and exposed, or at least expressed. The character has refused to take action while they weighed the risks, even briefly, and most likely have been persuaded to act either due to strong motivation or a mentor.

What's vital with the Action Taken phase is that the time of weighing and thinking and debating is over. For your story to move forward, the main character must take an action even if they are still unsure of the eventual outcome.

Often there's a Threshold Guardian character present in this area of your story. The Threshold Guardian is a character who can be positive (as in a loved one who wants to keep the protagonist from getting hurt if they do act) or negative (someone who doesn't want the character to move forward and change such as a bully, coworker, or rival) who wants the status quo to stay as is. They serve to block the protagonist from taking action and act as a first test in your character's commitment to change. Oftentimes this same character will be brought back later in the story as a way to show that they no longer can stop the protagonist because the protagonist has grown and changed so what once stopped them won't anymore. The Threshold Guardian does not need to be human, but can be an inanimate object—the first mountain to climb, a locked gate, a forbidden entrance that later in the story would never stop your character from moving forward.

> *Any scene that doesn't serve to—1) advance the plot, and/or—preferably* and *—2) deepen characterization will kill pacing. No matter how deliciously brilliant and lyrical a writer believes her prose is in that scene, she must be ruthless and cut it, or the reader will be bored and pacing will suffer.*
>
> —Alyssa Day, *New York Times* bestselling author of the Warriors of Poseidon series

If you are familiar with the three-act structure of story, first explained by Aristotle, this phase is the shift from the story setup, or Act I, to the heart of the story, which is Act II.

Examples of this Action Taken phase in movies will include when William Thacker (Hugh Grant) in *Notting Hill* tries to return Anna Scott's (Julia Roberts) phone call and must get past the hotel front desk (Threshold Guardian) by guessing her disguised name. Later in the story, this is repeated and the second time, William Thacker will not take a "no" when approaching a similar Threshold Guardian, which shows his Internal Character Growth.

In *An Officer and a Gentleman*, Zack Mayo (Richard Gere) meets Paula (Debra Winger) and spells out the ground rules for their relationship. When she accepts—Action Taken—they begin their relationship. The drill sergeant (Louis Gossett Jr.) acts most often as both Threshold Guardian and Mentor.

In *Men in Black*, James Edwards's (Will Smith's) Action Taken is when he passes the elderly man (not a major Threshold Guardian but still acting in the role) through the gates to the MIB Agency to become Agent J and assumes a new life that will forever change him.

The intention of this template is to make sure your character is acting vs. continuing to think or decide. You're also making sure that the action is well motivated. It must directly impact both the character's External Story Goal, as well as their Internal Character Growth. You, as the author, know about both the goal and the growth, whether the character does or not. Examples: In a mystery, your protagonist may think they are only seeking a few answers, not that they are going after a killer. In a romance, the heroine and hero may decide to combine forces in some way for an external reason, but they are not committing to a relationship in any way. So even if your character is unaware that this first step will lead them toward growth and change, you—as author—need to be aware that this change *must* occur. That's the reason for the questions asked in this template.

Note: The plotting templates are primarily filled out for main characters—the protagonists, antagonists, and villains, but can be used for secondary characters as well. Keep in mind that you give a character importance based on the number of pages in that character's POV, similar to how much screen time an actor has in a movie. You can fill out the templates for an antagonist, villain, or other secondary character even if you don't use the information in the story pages.

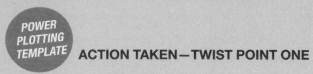

ACTION TAKEN—TWIST POINT ONE

The purpose of this template is to make sure that action is taken in the story and that it will impact both external events and internal character growth in some way. Tip: This is approximately a quarter to a third of the way into your story.

The Character for this template is:

----

1. What significant action happens (approximately a quarter to a third of the way into the story) that will change this character over the course of the story and how does this move the story forward?

   PLOT HOLE ALERT: If this happens too soon or too late in your story you risk either not enough story setup or not enough story development; also, if this is an action "thrown in" that does not move the story forward, then the plot is not holding up.

   ----

2. How does this action impact this character's overall External Story Goal (insert answer from Chapter 4)?

   ----

3. How does this action impact the character's Internal Character Growth (insert answer from Chapter 5)?

   ----

4. What tests will the character face to reach his or her External Story Goal or Internal Character Growth? (Name at least three—you can have more than three but at least three larger tests.)

----

5. Who will help this character reach his or her External Story Goal and how? (Name at least one.)

----

6. Who will hinder this character from reaching his or her External Story Goal and how? (Name at least one.)

POWER PLOTTING TIP A twist point is not a superficial surprise thrown in, but a change that creates a new question about the outcome of a story. It's also an opportunity for the protagonist to stop their attempt to move forward in the story, but because the character takes action, not only will they be changed, but also it will make it harder for them to return or revert to their Everyday World as they once were. In the movie *Gone with the Wind,* when Scarlett O'Hara confronts Ashley (the man she longs for) at a picnic about her feelings for him, he says he's bound to another woman; a conversation Rhett Butler overhears. The twist is that at the end of the picnic it's announced that war has broken out. Charles Hamilton, who she's been innocently flirting with, asks Scarlett to marry him before he goes to war, and she agrees.

The first twist is when Jason learns he's an assassin and has been framed for a murder.

1. **What significant action happens that will change this character over the course of the story and how does this move the story forward?**

   An African leader is assassinated and Jason learns he's an assassin and is being set up for the murder.

2. **How does this action impact this character's overall External Story Goal (to stop Treadstone)?**

   Jason realizes that the men after him are ruthless and will not hesitate to do anything to silence him.

3. **How does this action impact the character's Internal Character Growth (to accept his past and still believe he is a good man)?**

   Finding out Jason is an assassin takes him further away from accepting that he is a good man.

4. **What tests will the character face to reach his or her External Story Goal or Internal Character Growth? (Name at least three—you can have more than three but at least three larger tests.)**

   The African leader who might have had answers for Jason has been assassinated and Jason is framed. Jason must take Marie with him, which means he's responsible for another person. When faced with finding a place to hide, Jason's presence puts Marie's family in danger.

5. **Who will help this character reach his or her External Story Goal and how? (Name at least one.)**

   Marie is Jason's staunchest ally who pushes him to find out who he is and supports him regardless of each dark secret that is revealed about his past.

6. **Who will hinder this character from reaching his or her External Story Goal and how? (Name at least one.)**

   The CIA handler who initially wanted Bourne back in the fold but now wants him dead.

The first twist for Vivian is when she's denied entry into Edward's world.

1. **What significant action happens that will change this character over the course of the story and how does this move the story forward?**

   Vivian returns to Rodeo Drive with Edward and buys enough of a wardrobe to fit into his world for the week.

2. **How does this action impact this character's overall External Story Goal (to leave prostitution and find a more secure life)?**

   Now that Vivian looks as though she fits into Edward's world, her temporary security is better established.

3. **How does this action impact the character's Internal Character Growth (belief in herself and self worth)?**

   Because Vivian will be treated differently, she'll start to treat herself differently and begin to feel she is more than just a hooker.

4. **What tests will the character face to reach his or her External Story Goal or Internal Character Growth? (Name at least three—you can have more than three but at least three larger tests.)**

   Vivian must rub shoulders with the elite crowd at the polo match. She must deal with the lawyer finding out she is a hooker. She must deal with Edward's jealousy.

5. **Who will help this character reach his or her External Story Goal and how? (Name at least one.)**

   Edward will help Vivian, because he supports her masquerade. The hotel manager, because he champions her relationship with Edward as more than hooker and client.

6. **Who will hinder this character from reaching his or her External Story Goal and how? (Name at least one.)**

   The lawyer, because he wants Edward to return to the status quo and focus 100 percent on the next takeover deal; something that changed once Vivian came along.

The first twist for Edward is that he experiences a twinge of guilt over his business deal.

TIP: With two main character arcs happening in a romance, there can be more than one twist layered into the early part of the story.

1. **What significant action happens that will change this character over the course of the story and how does this move the story forward?**

   Because Edward caught himself being vulnerable to emotions when dealing with the grandfather figure, Edward redoubles his efforts to take over the company by calling in a favor from a senator to forestall a new contract to the firm that would allow the firm to avoid the hostile takeover.

2. **How does this action impact this character's overall External Story Goal (to make a partnership with a firm to grow and develop it instead of dismantling it)?**

   This brings Edward one step closer to closing the takeover deal and puts at risk his External Story Goal of buying to build.

3. **How does this action impact the character's Internal Character Growth (to be able to bond and emotionally connect with people)?**

   The action of having to acknowledge the grandfatherly business owner as being a man of integrity who cares for his family and employees puts Edward in conflict with his drive to remain emotionally unattached.

4. **What tests will the character face to reach his or her External Story Goal or Internal Character Growth? (Name at least three—you can have more than three but at least three larger tests.)**

    Edward will face jealousy over Vivian laughing and being comfortable with the grandfatherly businessman's handsome grandson. Edward will take Vivian to the opera to not only share with her but to please her, thinking of her needs over his own—a first for him. He will have to deal with wanting to spend time with Vivian when the attorney is pulling him back to the deal.

5. **Who will help this character reach his or her External Story Goal and how? (Name at least one.)**

    Vivian influences Edward to choose an alternative goal of buying and operating the company as a partner with the grandfatherly businessman.

6. **Who will hinder this character from reaching his or her External Story Goal now and how? (Name at least one.)**

    The lawyer who wants Edward to not change and continue to do business in the old way.

The first twist is when Ilsa shows up in his bar.

1. **What significant action happens that will change this character over the course of the story and how does this move the story forward?**

   Rick meets with Ilsa again privately.

2. **How does this action impact this character's overall External Story Goal (to remain neutral and not get involved in the struggle between resistance fighters and the Germans)?**

   Hurting over the breakup in Paris, Rick believes he can remain neutral until he discovers Ilsa's life is at stake if he doesn't act, and his life will be at stake if he does.

3. **How does this action impact the character's Internal Character Growth (to re-engage emotionally with life in order to make a commitment)?**

   Meeting with Ilsa is the first step toward Rick facing his past with her and reconnecting with his emotions.

4. **What tests will the character face to reach his or her External Story Goal or Internal Character Growth? (Name at least three—you can have more than three but at least three larger tests.)**

   After a drunken, bitter response to Ilsa's first explanation as to why she left him, Rick must reassure her that he does want to know what happened. He discovers that Ilsa is married, and was married when they knew each other in Paris. Rick must avoid having the police and Germans discover he has the Letters of Transit.

5. **Who will help this character reach his or her External Story Goal and how? (Name at least one.)**

   Captain Renault who feeds Rick key insights and information; Laszlo who acts as a role-model to Rick.

6. **Who will hinder this character from reaching his or her External Story Goal and how? (Name at least one.)**

   The German major who wants to stop Laszlo and does not care who else he takes down to do it.

The first twist is when Marlin encounters Dory and must act in spite of his fear.

1. What significant action happens that will change this character over the course of the story and how does this move the story forward?

   Marlin has gone after his son Nemo and is swimming in uncharted waters where he'll encounter danger.

2. How does this action impact this character's overall External Story Goal (to find his son)?

   It takes Marlin physically closer to finding Nemo.

3. How does this action impact the character's Internal Character Growth (to change his definition of what a good parent is from being overly protective to allowing his child to experience life)?

   It forces Marlin to experience life more fully; he can't cower at home in the comfortable setting he knows.

4. What tests will the character face to reach his or her External Story Goal or Internal Character Growth? (Name at least three—you can have more than three but at least three larger tests.)

   Marlin finds a facemask which might lead them to Nemo, but Marlin can't read what is written on it. An exploding submarine that almost ends his search. A school of stinging jellyfish that almost kills Dory, the only one Marlin trusts.

5. Who will help this character reach his or her External Story Goal and how? (Name at least one.)

   Dory, who by remaining with Marlin and reading the address on the facemask, gives them a valuable clue as to where Nemo has been taken. The pelican that connects Marlin's quest with the new fish in the dentist's tank.

6. Who will hinder this character from reaching his or her External Story Goal and how? (Name at least one.)

   The sharks when they smell blood. The fish with the headlights. The jellyfish that almost kills Dory.

9 POWER PLOTTING
Secondary Story Initiated —
Test Your Premise

*"To make a strong story, all the subplots should connect back
to the main story line."*
—Bob Mayer, *NYT* best-selling author of *Don't Look Down*

Many writers want to know the most logical place to start a Subplot or
Secondary Story Line in a different character's POV that will directly
impact the primary story line. Just after the Action Taken is such a
place. You can foreshadow the Subplot earlier in some way, but make
sure that the reader is hooked enough into the primary story line that
they are willing to wait and pick up that central story again if you
do shift focus. Once action has been taken in the primary story line
(Chapter 8), a large story question is raised: Will they succeed in overcoming their first test to reaching that goal? After you've raised that
question you can segue to your Subplot or Secondary Story Line.

Test Your Premise involves the obstacles or tests you will have
your character engage in to show the reader that even as the character encounters these setbacks he or she will continue forward to achieve
the Character's next Immediate External Goal or the External Story
Goal. These tests will be the meat of your book from about a quarter to a third of the way through the story up through the middle, and

sometimes a little beyond. They serve to show Internal Character Growth by facing obstacles and fear in small increments. These tests also allow your character to find allies who can help them toward their External Story Goal and discover enemies who will be acting to stop them.

In *An Officer and a Gentleman*, Zach Mayo was able to immediately stand out physically in his group of officer cadets because of his street background and training. However, he faltered when it came to academic proficiency, so he has to make an ally to tutor him. He also faces Tests in dealing with drunken locals (enemies), learns how to support his cadet peers (allies), has his stash of contraband goods discovered by the drill sergeant, and learns how to have a best friend—something that quickly becomes apparent he's never had before. All of these Tests prepare Zach to better to handle the Stakes Raised (Chapter 11) and his Transformation (Chapter 13).

> *The key to a powerful plot is powerhouse brainstorming—immerse yourself in creating your characters' world until you see the potential for plot twists in even the heroine's bowl of potpourri.*
>
> —Catherine Mann, best-selling author of military romantic suspense

The intention of this template is to clarify at least three Tests your protagonist will experience as he or she moves toward a Character's Immediate External Goal, which in turn brings a character closer to their External Story Goal that you, as the author, know. Passing and surviving these Tests will also bring your protagonist closer to Internal Character Growth. Watch for potential allies or enemies your protagonist will face through this section of your story. This template will help you identify where and how to introduce and weave in a strong Subplot or a Secondary Story Line.

Note: Your protagonist will be the one facing the Tests. In a romance or any genre where you have two protagonists—your hero and heroine—one can have larger Tests than the other, but the Tests will most likely (though not always) impact both characters, although possibly in different ways (see examples from *Pretty Woman*). If you are using the template to answer questions for a villain, be aware the villain will not be experiencing Internal Character Growth as they will not change over the course of the story.

SECONDARY STORY INITIATED—TEST YOUR PREMISE

The purpose of this template is to determine if the Subplot impacts the primary story or if the Secondary Story Line mirrors the primary story. Tip: A Secondary Story Line will enhance a story or add texture, but can be removed without real damage to the plot. But a Subplot should be so important to the central plot that if it is removed, the story will fall apart.

The Character for this template is:

----

1. What three tests will this character experience in trying to reach his or her External Story Goal or Internal Character Growth?

   TIP: These can be the same three from previous templates and should be large enough tests to fill your manuscript from a quarter of the way into the story until at least halfway or beyond.

   ----

2. Is there a Subplot or Secondary Story Line? If so, what is it?

   TIP: If you have a Subplot, add how the story's Primary Story Line will fall apart without the Subplot so that you can confirm it is not just a Secondary Story Line.

   ----

3. If so, which characters are involved in the Subplot or Secondary Story Line?

   ----

4. How do the actions of the characters in the Subplot "impact" the Primary Story Line or how do the actions of the characters in the Secondary Story Line mirror the Primary Story Line?

_____

_____

_____

POWER PLOTTING TIP Most larger stories (over 80,000 words) will have a Subplot running concurrently with the primary story line. The key to weaving this in is to make sure your additional plots and story lines tie into the Primary Story Line and that the supporting characters involved do not overpower the main character's story arc. (Note: The larger your book the more Subplots and Secondary Story Lines you can include in your story.) In *Star Wars*, Luke Skywalker is on a Primary Story Line of discovery about his father, but his need to find the answers becomes entwined with the secondary plot, which is Princess Leia's battle with the Empire to save her people.

1. **What three tests will this character experience in trying to reach his or her External Story Goal or Internal Character Growth?**

   The African leader who might have answers is assassinated before Jason can speak with him. Jason and Marie are chased through Paris by the police after an assassin attacks him in his apartment. They have to rely on Marie to find a safe place to hide because Jason has no idea where to go to be safe and this action, hiding out at her half-brother's farmhouse, risks innocent people including children.

2. **Is there a Subplot or Secondary Story Line? If so, what is it?**

   The Subplot is the confrontation between the CIA handler and his boss back at CIA headquarters, and their need to silence Jason rather than risk intel getting out about a covert operation gone bad where trained assassins had been created to use against heads of state of other countries. This Subplot is why Jason is racing to find out who he is since this group represents a very real danger to his existence. Without this Subplot Jason would simply be a man trying to figure out his real identity.

3. **If so which characters are involved in the Subplot or Secondary Story Line?**

   The CIA handler and his boss.

4. **How do the actions of the characters in the Subplot impact the Primary Story Line or how do the actions of the characters in the Secondary Story Line mirror the Primary Story Line?**

   If the CIA succeed with their goal—of eliminating Bourne to protect themselves—then Bourne and Marie must die. It ramps up the need for Bourne to find out who he is and what happened to him that caused his memory loss in order to protect himself.

1. **What three tests will this character experience in trying to reach his or her External Story Goal or Internal Character Growth?**

   Vivian must rub shoulders with the elite crowd at the polo match. She must deal with the fallout of Edward's jealousy (when he tells the lawyer she is a hooker after seeing her talk to the young guy at the polo match). She will have to choose between Edward offering her the chance to live in luxury as his mistress or admitting she wants him in a real relationship (marriage), which will mean her walking away.

2. **Is there a Subplot or Secondary Story Line? If so, what is it?**

   The Subplot is Edward's business deal to take over the family-owned company so he can dismantle it. This Subplot is at the center of what Edward believes is his goal—to dismantle a company. The Subplot also provides the arena for Vivian's change as well, since she is forced to make changes due to being his companion at social events. (There is another less significant Subplot: Vivian's trouble with the drug dealer, which provides motivation for Vivian to agree to Edward's deal for a week, but the Subplot surrounding Edward's business deal is the stronger of the two.)

3. **If so, which characters are involved in the Subplot or Secondary Story Line?**

   Edward and the grandfatherly businessman.

4. **How do the actions of the characters in the Subplot impact the Primary Story Line or how do the actions of the characters in the Secondary Story Line mirror the Primary Story Line?**

   Playing a high-stakes tug of war over a forty-year-old shipping business. Edward's ruthlessness in business shows what he's willing to do to get what he wants regardless of the emotional costs to others. It is this behavior that must change if he wants to have a long-term relationship. Through the parallel plot of the business negotiations, Edward and Vivian's relationship is drawn to the forefront and becomes more important than the business deal.

131

1. What three tests will this character experience in trying to reach his or her External Story Goal or Internal Character Growth?

   Edward will face his jealousy over Vivian laughing and talking privately with the grandfatherly businessman's handsome grandson. He will take Vivian to the opera to not only share with her but to please her, thinking of her needs over his own—a first for him. He will agree to spend a day off with Vivian instead of going into the office where his attorney is waiting for him to work on the business deal.

   NOTE: Because this is a romance, the answers for questions 2–5 are the same information for Edward's template as on Vivian's template. In a romance, by this point in the story the two main characters' actions and decisions impact each other; therefore, one template will impact the other.

1. **What three tests will this character experience in trying to reach his or her External Story Goal or Internal Character Growth?**

   After a drunken, bitter response to Ilsa's first overture of explanation as to why she left him in Paris, Rick must reassure her that he does want to know what happened and why. He discovers that Ilsa is married, and was married when they knew each other in Paris, to Laszlo, a freedom fighter Rick secretly admires. Rick must avoid having the police and Germans discover that he has the Letters of Transit.

2. **Is there a Subplot or Secondary Story Line? If so, what is it?**

   The Subplot is Rick and Ilsa's love affair and relationship, which drives Rick's motivation to help Ilsa and her husband in the end.

3. **If so, which characters are involved in the Subplot or Secondary Story Line?**

   Rick and Ilsa and her husband Laszlo.

4. **How do the actions of the characters in the Subplot impact the Primary Story Line or how do the actions of the characters in the Secondary Story Line mirror the Primary Story Line?**

   Rick makes overtures to Ilsa so that he can try to understand what happened in Paris but she makes it clear that she doesn't believe he's the same man or that he's capable of understanding. Yet each step Rick takes toward Ilsa increases Rick's feelings for her and unleashes his dormant support of the underdog—which will draw him into the conflict between the resistance fighters and the Germans, jeopardizing his ability to remain neutral.

1. **What three tests will this character experience in trying to reach his or her External Story Goal or Internal Character Growth?**

   Marlin finds a facemask which might lead him and Dory to Nemo, but Marlin can't read what's written on the mask. He has to deal with an exploding submarine that almost kills Marlin and Dory. They also encounter a school of stinging jellyfish that almost kill Dory, the only friend he has at this point.

2. **Is there a Subplot or Secondary Story Line? If so, what is it?**

   The Secondary Story Line is Nemo's experience in the tank of fish in the dentist's office. (Note: This is clearly a Secondary Story Line that adds texture to the overall story, but does not impact the central plot, which is for Marlin to find and rescue his son. If we don't see what goes on in the aquarium, the primary story line remains constant.)

3. **If so, which characters are involved in the Subplot or Secondary Story Line?**

   Nemo, the other fish in the aquarium, and the dentist.

4. **How do the actions of the characters in the Subplot impact the Primary Story Line or how do the actions of the characters in the Secondary Story Line mirror the Primary Story Line?**

   One of the other fish convinces Nemo to try and escape the tank and gives him information about how this can be done. Under the mentorship of this fish, Nemo learns to be proactive in protecting his own life instead of simply being afraid and powerless, which will aid him when he and his father are reunited and mirrors the lessons Marlin is learning.

Roget's Thesaurus says **conflict** means "Opposition; disagreement; battle; to oppose or vie."

10 POWER PLOTTING
Things Are about to Get Far Worse

> "You can spend a lot of time developing characters, but unless they come into conflict that will test them, there's nothing interesting happening."
>
> —Tom Schulman, Screenwriter of
> *What About Bob?* and *Dead Poets Society*

This is a key area in your novel that many writers either ignore or rush through, but by slowing your story here and allowing your readers to catch their breath, you are able to set up the next phase—Stakes Raised: Twist Point Two—in a way that maximizes the middle of your novel. This does not mean that you bog down your pacing. This area must still remain active.

Things Are about to Get Far Worse is where you can show through the results of testing of your premise (Chapter 9 was where you allowed your protagonist to face obstacles and overcome them, identify enemies, and meet new allies) that your protagonist has become somewhat comfortable, believing he or she can face whatever they must face next. The protagonist's awareness of his or her External Story Goal may be morphing here and becoming clearer if the character has only been focused on each Immediate External Goal up to this point. In addition, the character feels stronger in the ability to overcome whatever troubles arise next.

During this resting point in a romance, your characters will probably be adjusting to the concept of having a relationship. They haven't necessarily acknowledged that they might be in love, or want to love again, but they are more comfortable with elements of the relationship such as having someone to come home to or to support them or to be part of a couple. In a mystery, this part of the story is where the sleuth feels he or she might have a handle on who committed a crime or why it was committed and have even eliminated some potential suspects. In a sci-fi story, the protagonist has adjusted to the new environment or world, or adjusted to dealing with any new threats.

Think of this phase as that comfortable I've-got-this-figured-out experience when people have settled into a new job after three months. They've made new friends, know who to steer clear of, and think they have a handle on their work, but right around the corner is an unexpected challenge they must face that puts their job at risk if they fail.

This is where Anna Scott and William Thacker have had a light, carefree date in *Notting Hill,* and she asks him up to her hotel room.

In *Bridget Jones's Diary*, this is the part where Mark Darcy comes to Bridget's flat and makes dinner with her, and then stays to meet and enjoy her friends.

One of the key elements of this area of your story is that the protagonist is more often than not under an illusion, thinking things are one way, but are about to find out differently. Think Maggie Carpenter (Julia Roberts) and Ike Graham (Richard Gere) in *Runaway Bride.* This phase was the lighthearted, fun segment where they had committed to getting married, but it's an illusion. Maggie has never faced what has kept her from the altar up to this point and Ike is ignoring the reasons behind why Maggie has run before. Until those reasons are faced, it's most likely she will run again.

Another nuance of this phase is having your protagonist get into the mind of the opponent, whether the opponent is an antagonist or a villain.

In the novel *Pride and Prejudice,* this is where Fitzwilliam Darcy and Elizabeth Bennet have appeared to reconcile at his estate and all seems well until Elizabeth receives word that her sister has eloped with Mr. George Wickham. This is a social disaster for her and her family that also appears to create a gulf between her and Darcy (illusion). In reality Darcy finds himself having to think like Wickham in order to find him and force him to marry Elizabeth's sister; this is Darcy's way of helping Elizabeth.

In mystery novels, the sleuth can start thinking more like the killer; in romance novels, the hero or heroine can start realizing and understanding more about the other one; in sci-fi novels, the protagonist can start accepting and seeing the new world from the view of insiders in a way that seemed impossible when the story started.

This area of your story is rich with character development, clarifying that there is still risk for your character, raising the stakes and conflict—all of which help to reveal what's at stake if your protagonist fails during Stakes Raised (Chapter 11) in your story.

This template is leading up to the middle of your story and the intention of this template is to give a breathing point before the stakes in the story are raised. It's also to clarify illusions, emotions, and motivations of your characters that will propel them into the second half of their story.

THINGS ARE ABOUT TO GET FAR WORSE

The purpose for this template is to set up raising the stakes as you head toward the midpoint of your story.

The Character for this template is:

----

1. What is this Character's Immediate External Goal that he or she is striving for at this point (leading up to the midpoint of the story)?

----

2. What will reaching this Character's Immediate External Goal mean to this character?

----

3. What is this character hoping will happen if he or she reaches this Immediate External Goal?

----

4. How does this character feel as he or she approaches the most Immediate External Goal?

----

5. What will happen if this character doesn't reach this Immediate External Goal?

----

6. Does this character have any illusions about reaching his or her External Story Goal or the meaning of his or her External Story Goal? (In other words, the illusion is that the character thinks if he or she reached this next Immediate External Goal, that all will be fine.) If so, what is the illusion?

----

7. Who else is involved at this point in your story? How and why?

POWER PLOTTING TIP It isn't enough that a character is still striving for a goal. There have to be enough roadblocks thrown in the character's path to make the goal worth achieving. As the challenges and obstacles grow, the reader will engage deeper with the character and want the character to reach his or her goal. We cheer for people who succeed against all odds.

1. What is this Character's Immediate External Goal that he or she is striving for at this point?

   For Jason to reach a safe place to hide while he figures out how to make himself and Marie disappear from the powerful people chasing them.

2. What will reaching this Character's Immediate External Goal mean to this character?

   Security, even temporarily.

3. What is this character hoping will happen if he or she reaches this Immediate External Goal?

   That he has some time to think and regroup and plan how to hide deeper from those trying to neutralize him and Marie.

4. How does this character feel as he or she approaches the most Immediate External Goal?

   Jason feels concerned for Marie's safety, but he feels a measure of relief that they have escaped the police and his unknown enemy's dragnet for the moment.

5. What will happen if this character doesn't reach this Immediate External Goal?

   Both Jason and Marie will likely be killed.

6. Does this character have any illusions about reaching his or her External Story Goal or the meaning of his or her External Story Goal?

   Yes, while Jason knows he's a former assassin, he has no idea of the breadth and scope of the threat against him nor the measures his pursuers are willing to employ to stop him and her because of her association with him.

7. Who else is involved at this point in your story? How and why?

   Marie, because she's cast her lot in with Jason. The CIA handler who is trying to stop the threat of Jason exposing the Treadstone Project.

1. **What is this Character's Immediate External Goal that he or she is striving for at this point?**

   Vivian's goal is to fit into Edward's world for a week, but to remain emotionally uninvolved.

2. **What will reaching this Character's Immediate External Goal mean to this character?**

   That Vivian can walk away with the security of the money Edward will pay her and not get her heart broken.

3. **What is this character hoping will happen if he or she reaches this Immediate External Goal?**

   Vivian is hoping she will feel safe when she returns to the only way of life she knows, that of a hooker.

4. **How does this character feel as he or she approaches the most Immediate External Goal?**

   Vivian is feeling confident about the progress she's made to fit into Edward's world, but also insecure as she realizes her belonging is not forever.

5. **What will happen if this character doesn't reach this Immediate External Goal?**

   If Vivian fails to fit into Edward's world, she knows he is a shrewd businessman so she expects he will not pay the entire amount due, which would leave her and her roommate at the mercy of a vicious drug dealer.

6. **Does this character have any illusions about reaching his or her External Story Goal or the meaning of his or her External Story Goal?**

   Yes, Vivian is hiding from the fact she's already in love with Edward. So she's acting as if it's business as usual while falling deeper in love every day.

7. **Who else is involved at this point in your story? How and why?**

   Edward, who is opening up emotionally to her. Vivian's roommate who advises Vivian to cut and run.

1. **What is this Character's Immediate External Goal that he or she is striving for at this point?**

   Edward is maneuvering to take over the family-owned business on his terms and moving in for the kill, so his goal is to win the tug-of-war he's in with the grandfatherly man who owns the business Edward wants.

2. **What will reaching this Character's Immediate External Goal mean to this character?**

   Just another win in Edward's business life, his measure of success.

3. **What is this character hoping will happen if he or she reaches this Immediate External Goal?**

   Edward hopes he'll be able to close the deal and move on without feeling remorse so he can get back to business as usual.

4. **How does this character feel as he or she approaches the most Immediate External Goal?**

   Edward is having second thoughts about the business deal.

5. **What will happen if this character doesn't reach this Immediate External Goal?**

   For Edward, failing to take over this company will mean he has lost a battle and his reputation of being a ruthless businessman will suffer.

6. **Does this character have any illusions about reaching his or her External Story Goal or the meaning of his or her External Story Goal?**

   He believes he can get involved with Vivian and doing so won't impact his business life or his personal life.

7. **Who else is involved at this point in your story? How and why?**

   Vivian, because she is forcing him to look at his life. The lawyer, who is pushing to return to the status quo. The grandfatherly man who is treating Edward with the respect Edward never received from his father.

1. **What is this Character's Immediate External Goal that he or she is striving for at this point?**

   Rick is trying to talk to Ilsa to find out what he wouldn't let her tell him the night before. He's also avoiding the French police who are searching his club for the Letters of Transit.

2. **What will reaching this Character's Immediate External Goal mean to this character?**

   Talking to Ilsa is Rick's attempt to make up for acting so badly previously. Avoiding the police is part of his neutrality policy.

3. **What is this character hoping will happen if he or she reaches this Immediate External Goal?**

   If Rick talks to Ilsa he's hoping he can understand what happened in the past, maybe even make a difference with her now. Avoiding the police means Rick can continue to straddle the noncommitment line and he will be able to avoid taking a side in the war around him.

4. **How does this character feel as he or she approaches the most Immediate External Goal?**

   That Rick stands to lose something important if he simply lets Ilsa walk out of his life again. And that he is still safe as long as he avoids choosing a side between the Germans and the Resistance movement, which means he'll escape the war unscathed.

5. **What will happen if this character doesn't reach this Immediate External Goal?**

    If he lets Ilsa walk away without finding out what happened in Paris, he'll never have peace of mind, closure, nor healing. If he fails to remain neutral in the political conflict, he's doomed to get burned either by the Germans if their power increases, which it looks like it will, or by those who feel passionately about fighting the Germans.

6. **Does this character have any illusions about reaching his or her External Story Goal or the meaning of his or her External Story Goal?**

    Yes, Rick's illusion is that if he understands why Ilsa left him in Paris, then he will stop loving her and that as long as he remains neutral, he will never have to make a stand as to whether he is pro-German or anti-German.

7. **Who else is involved at this point in your story? How and why?**

    Ilsa, because Rick indicates he's willing to listen to her now, which means their relationship is still viable. Victor Laszlo, who needs the Letters of Transit in Rick's possession and is actively working toward getting them. The French Captain Renault, who is juggling pressure from the German major to move against Laszlo and stands to hurt Ilsa in the process.

THINGS ARE ABOUT TO GET FAR WORSE MOVIE EXAMPLE:
Finding Nemo

THE CHARACTER FOR THIS TEMPLATE IS:
Marlin (Nemo's father)

1. **What is this Character's Immediate External Goal that he or she is striving for at this point?**

    Thanks to help from the turtles, Marlin and Dory are closer to Sydney, but now they are lost. Dory is calling to a whale to ask directions, but Marlin's immediate goal is to stop her.

2. **What will reaching this Character's Immediate External Goal mean to this character?**

    Marlin fears that if Dory brings in the wrong type of fish there will be trouble, so convincing her to stop seeking help and trusting everyone will keep them safe—in his mind.

3. **What is this character hoping will happen if he or she reaches this Immediate External Goal?**

    Marlin hopes he and Dory can find Sydney, Australia (where Nemo is supposed to be), on their own.

4. **How does this character feel as he or she approaches the most Immediate External Goal?**

    Very worried, because he can't stop Dory.

5. **What will happen if this character doesn't reach this Immediate External Goal?**

    If Marlin and Dory don't find directions, they may never get to Sydney and save Nemo.

6. **Does this character have any illusions about reaching his or her External Story Goal or the meaning of his or her External Story Goal?**

    Yes, Marlin's illusion is that all he has to do is get to Sydney to find Nemo. Marlin thinks rescuing Nemo will be easy from that point forward.

7. **Who else is involved at this point in your story? How and why?**

    · Dory, who decides to ask a whale for directions to teach Marlin that not all risks are bad.

11 POWER PLOTTING
Stakes Raised—Twist Point Two

> "Try to get your characters into interesting trouble. Allow your characters to misbehave. Let them stay out after 11."
> —Charles Baxter,
> author of *The Soul Thief* and *Feast of Love*

Congratulations, you have analyzed and plotted up to the midpoint in your story. This is a major twist point of the story, but not to be confused with the Transformation, which happens later (Chapter 13).

At Twist Point Two your story will change direction once again. It's an opportunity for your protagonist to stop striving for their external goal, to give up or turn back. You've clarified (Chapter 10) that there are good reasons for your protagonist to stay where they are and remain with their illusions. But your character won't stop here. He or she will move forward, forever changed.

The function of this part of your story is to face a death of some sort, which will force your protagonists to face the fact that they can never go back to the way they were at the beginning of the story. When you think of death, think in terms of the death of a relationship, of a dream, of a belief that no longer serves the character. A virgin who makes love for the first time deals with a death of his or her innocence, a battle scene that may be won still shows death on a massive scale, a

146

friendship forever broken is a death. The death can be physical (as in somebody dies or almost dies), metaphoric, or symbolic.

When you think life or death, this is in terms of what's life or death for your protagonist. So even in a lighter book, such as a comedy, the death of a dream or a relationship or an illusion can still have devastating impact and change your character's outlook on his or her world.

A key method to show the ramifications of this Twist Point is to use other characters who clarify and act as the reader in identifying with your protagonist regarding what's been lost. The best friend or a group of friends or anyone you choose can be the ones who empathize or speak aloud or focus in on the sense of loss and death here. The reader must experience the change and loss in order to appreciate the sweetness of life beyond this point.

> *Having a well developed character and story "blueprint" makes the writing experience faster and more enjoyable.*
>
> —Mae Nunn, award-winning author of the popular Texas Treasure series

Examples of Twist Point Two in movies:

In *Men in Black*, Twist Point Two is when the alien creature gets to the NYC morgue before Agents J and K and not only finds the most immediate External Story Goal—the galaxy—but takes the deputy medical examiner hostage, which creates both escalating stakes in the External Story Goal (protect the world), but also creates immediate personal stakes for Agent J (save the girl).

In *Bridget Jones's Diary*, this is where Bridget says "no" to Daniel Cleaver's offer of getting back together—an offer she would have jumped at earlier in the story. Mark Darcy also walks away, so now she faces the death of two relationships. However, she must face them, and face her own actions that created the situations, before she is ready to accept a relationship with a good, decent man.

The intention of this template is to make sure that a dramatic change has occurred and thus the protagonist or protagonists will never be the same again. It's also meant to make sure the stakes are raised in your story and that there will be ramifications due to the actions that were taken and experienced here.

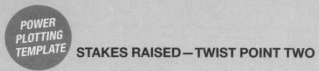

POWER PLOTTING TEMPLATE

STAKES RAISED—TWIST POINT TWO

The purpose of this template is to determine if your story is escalating (yes) or remaining static (no).

The Character for this template is:

----

1. What event (external test) does this character face in the middle of the story that changes the direction of the story?

----

2. Before the event in question 1 above, how did this character feel about facing it?

----

3. What is the outcome of that event (external test) and what changes happen as a result?

----

4. How does this character feel about the outcome of that event and the changes?

----

5. How have the stakes in the story been raised?

   ----

6. What Aftermath happens as a result of Twist Point Two and Raising the Stakes?

   ----

1. **What event (external test) does this character face in the middle of the story that changes the direction of the story?**

   An assassin locates Jason and Marie in the farmhouse.

2. **Before the event in question 1 above, how did this character feel about facing it?**

   Jason was under the illusion that if he simply ran far enough and hid deep enough, he might stay safe and keep his past in the past.

3. **What is the outcome of that event (external test) and what changes happen as a result?**

   Jason goes on the offense instead of the defense.

4. **How does this character feel about the outcome of that event and the changes?**

   Jason accepts that he cannot hide. He must face his past head-on and go toward the threat instead of running from it. That's the only way to protect Marie and give both of them a chance at a future.

5. **How have the stakes in the story been raised?**

   Jason has put other innocent people at risk who could die because of him if he does not stop the CIA threat. The CIA stands to not only lose Jason but risks exposure of this top-secret program if Jason is not killed.

6. **What Aftermath happens as a result of Twist Point Two and Raising the Stakes?**

   Because her safety outweighs her aid to him, Jason sends Marie away to Greece. Then Jason returns to Paris to confront his former CIA handler.

1. **What event (external test) does this character face in the middle of the story that changes the direction of the story?**

    Vivian must attend a polo match where she'll have to interact with Edward's peers, plus face Edward's lawyer who lets her know he knows she's only a hooker.

2. **Before the event in question 1 above, how did this character feel about facing it?**

    Because she has the clothes and has passed one test—dinner with the grandfatherly businessman and his grandson—Vivian's more comfortable as Edward's date. She is nervous, but enjoying herself at the polo match initially.

3. **What is the outcome of that event (external test) and what changes happen as a result?**

    After seeing Vivian laughing with the grandson, Edward lets the lawyer know she's a hooker and not an industrial spy. Then the lawyer approaches Vivian as a hooker, embarrassing her and undermining her confidence.

4. **How does this character feel about the outcome of that event and the changes?**

    Vivian feels deeply betrayed by Edward and surprised that he'd pimp her services to his lawyer.

5. **How have the stakes in the story been raised?**

    Vivian realizes she can be hurt emotionally by Edward and Edward realizes he has become emotionally attached to Vivian in spite of their business arrangement.

6. **What Aftermath happens as a result of Twist Point Two and Raising the Stakes?**

    Edward keeps Vivian from leaving him and apologizes, a first for him, and admits he was jealous, another first for him. He tells her he wants to make up for the incident by taking her out to the opera—sharing something very personal to him with her.

1. **What event (external test) does this character face in the middle of the story that changes the direction of the story?**

    At the polo match, Edward becomes jealous after seeing Vivian laughing with someone he perceives as a rival—the businessman's grandson. Edward is faced with having to control his emotions.

2. **Before the event in question 1 above, how did this character feel about facing it?**

    Before the match it was easier for Edward to view Vivian as an asset he could use to win the business deal, so he's feeling confident about attending with her.

3. **What is the outcome of that event (external test) and what changes happen as a result?**

    Edward becomes jealous of another man showing attention to Vivian, an alien feeling for him and in a backlash against the strong emotion; he reveals Vivian's true occupation to his lawyer.

4. **How does this character feel about the outcome of that event and the changes?**

    Edward realizes his actions, or knee-jerk emotional reaction, led to the lawyer's hitting on Vivian. Edward is truly sorry for putting her in that position.

5. **How have the stakes in the story been raised?**

    Edward realizes he's falling for Vivian and that's dangerous territory for him. He's not self-confident when it comes to relationships and he has no intention of being hurt again, but he doesn't want to lose her.

6. **What Aftermath happens as a result of Twist Point Two and raising the stakes?**

    Edward keeps Vivian from leaving him and decides to take Vivian to the opera as an act of atonement. It's his way of opening up and sharing a private part of himself with her, showing her she is special to him.

Casablanca

THE CHARACTER FOR THIS TEMPLATE IS:
Richard "Rick" Blaine (Humphrey Bogart)

1. **What event (external test) does this character face in the middle of the story that changes the direction of the story?**

   Laszlo makes a mockery of the Germans by having patrons of Rick's club sing the French national anthem louder than the Germans are singing the German national anthem. This shows increasing tensions between the anti-Germans and the Germans, soon to reach a crisis point. When asked what Rick will take for the Letters of Transit, Rick refuses any price and tells Laszlo curtly to ask his wife Ilsa why.

2. **Before the event in question 1 above, how did this character feel about facing it?**

   Rick was hoping to avoid a direct confrontation between the anti-German and pro-German patrons of his club. Since Rick only recently found out that Ilsa was Laszlo's wife, Rick is still reeling from the news that, when they were together in Paris, she was already married to a man Rick personally admires as a patriot.

3. **What is the outcome of that event (external test) and what changes happen as a result?**

   The Germans decide to more aggressively contain Laszlo, putting his and Ilsa's lives at risk. Rick has taken one step closer to non-neutrality by letting Laszlo lead the French singers when the band actually looks to Rick for approval before playing and Rick nods, not just allowing it, but authorizing the singing and as a result his café is shut down. Rick facing Laszlo means that Laszlo cannot hide from the fact that Ilsa and Rick were more than friends who knew each other in Paris.

4. **How does this character feel about the outcome of that event and the changes?**

   Rick still thinks he can avoid too much personal or professional damage (even though his club is shut down for a short time). By bringing Laszlo into the relationship triangle, Rick pushes Ilsa to make a choice between Laszlo and him.

5. **How have the stakes in the story been raised?**

   The Germans are more desperate to stop Laszlo's influence in Casablanca. Ilsa is more determined than ever to see Laszlo safe and to find a way to be with Rick.

6. **What aftermath happens as a result of Twist Point Two and raising the stakes?**

   Ilsa approaches Rick in his café, demanding the Letters of Transit at gunpoint.

1. **What event (external test) does this character face in the middle of the story that changes the direction of the story?**

   Marlin and Dory are swallowed by a whale.

2. **Before the event in question 1 above, how did this character feel about facing it?**

   He's still afraid to trust that the world is not a big, bad, scary place, so he's terrified of meeting up with the whale, which represents a big, scary threat.

3. **What is the outcome of that event (external test) and what changes happen as a result?**

   Marlin trusts Dory and follows her lead, releasing his death grip on the whale's tongue and falling down to what Marlin believes is their doom but instead of dying the whale blows them out of his blowhole and they are that much closer to Sydney, Australia and thus Nemo.

4. **How does this character feel about the outcome of that event and the changes?**

   Marlin is overjoyed that not only did they survive, but that Dory was right when she told him sometimes you just have to have faith and good things can happen.

5. **How have the stakes in the story been raised?**

   Both Marlin and Dory are now close to Sydney and have the chance to save Nemo.

6. **What Aftermath happens as a result of Twist Point Two and raising the stakes?**

   They are befriended by a pelican who knows where Nemo is, and the pelican brings Dory and Marlin to Nemo.

According to <u>Roget's Thesaurus</u>, **aftermath** means "Consequence; result; outcome; finale; payoff."

12 POWER PLOTTING
Aftermath—Regrouping/Decision

"While we are free to choose our actions, we are not free to choose the consequences of our actions."
—Stephen R. Covey, author of
The Seven Habits of Highly Effective People®

As a pacing device, this area of your story—after the Stakes Raised (Chapter 11)—can be manifested so many different ways on the page.

This can be a strong high-five moment—that brief moment where the protagonist and other characters feel emotional catharsis. That all the pain experienced up to this point was worth the struggle. The story is not yet over, but for a brief shining period, life feels good in large part because your protagonist faced death in some version in the last phase. In romances, this is often where the hero and heroine will make love, or make love in a different way than when they started their relationship.

In *Top Gun*, Maverick (Tom Cruise) and Charlie (Kelly McGillis) make love after Maverick's near-death experience as a fighter pilot—his Twist Point Two. Not all is well for him—his best friend died because of his actions, his career is in jeopardy, but he's grown a lot as a person (Internal Character Growth) and learned about humility due to loss (death and near-death). As a result, he's earned a true relationship with Charlie.

This area of your story can be a reflective time, a reviewing of what's been done and accomplished, again with other characters to attest to the efforts expended thus far and the high-five being experienced. In the movie *S.W.A.T.*, this is the scene where the group of new and reinstated SWAT members is enjoying a celebration at a pizza restaurant. They have passed the exercise they were expected to fail and have become official SWAT members. While they know there is danger and risk ahead, they have no idea how much danger and how personal the next area of the story—Transformation (Chapter 13)—will be.

In *Galaxy Quest*, this is the area of the story where the actors-turned-real-warriors have destroyed the alien vessel and appear to have defeated the villains. They gather on the deck of the spacecraft, just as they used to gather in the same place when they were filming their TV show; only now they have truly fought the good fight and survived. They are forever changed and know this, but they are all alive, though others died.

The area of your story that can go hand in hand with Aftermath is the Regrouping/Decision element. While many times combined in story structure these two areas of your story serve different story functions. The Regrouping/Decision separates Act II of the three-act structure from Act III—the Resolution of your story.

The function of the upcoming resolution (Chapter 14) is to clarify to a reader that while the lessons learned and experienced thus far in the story allowed your protagonist to survive Twist Point Two (Chapter 11) in order to make sure that those lessons have been mastered and not just learned, a few more steps must be met and conquered.

Here, in Aftermath and Regrouping/Decision is when the mountain climber, who has come a long way from the plains and viewing the mountain from far away, now must conquer the final ascent, the final peak in order to reach the top of the mountain. He or she must conquer the peak, then return in some way to the plains and share what he or she has earned or learned with others.

In Regrouping/Decision, the protagonist is once again given an opportunity to stop and turn back. Reasons are presented and weighed. Here a Threshold Guardian can be interjected, but this time the protagonist will handle this obstacle in a different way than before (Chapter 8) as a way to show character growth and change.

Many times the Regrouping/Decision is shown as an actual physical process—the protagonist is already returning to his or her Everyday World unaware or aware that one more huge test must be faced.

In *Galaxy Quest,* this is where the actor-crew leave their new friends and return to earth, but re-entering the earth's atmosphere and landing still poses challenges and risks and the story isn't quite over.

In *Bridget Jones's Diary,* this is where Bridget has returned at Christmastime to her parents' home, an echo of how the movie started. Only this time, she discovers that Mark Darcy is once again at his parents' home and she'll have a chance to talk with him. So she hops in her car and races over snowy lanes to reach him, unaware that he's about to leave for America.

In the *Chronicles of Riddick,* this is where Riddick and others, including Kyria, the girl he rescued from jail, are racing across the planet Crematoria before the sun comes up and fries everyone. Riddick's Twist Point Two (Chapter 11) is the race across the planet, with the assumption that once he and Kyria reached the cave containing the spaceship to take them off the planet all would be well. Instead they had to fight their way into the cave where Riddick battled with a warrior sent by the leader of the Necromongers. Riddick is left for dead and Kyria is taken hostage by the Necromongers: In the Aftermath, Riddick is saved by another Necromonger named Flurion. Flurion gives him the information and the motivation (Regrouping/Decision) to rescue Kyria. That is how Riddick comes up against what he's avoided so far (the External Story Goal established by the author)—fighting the Necromongers directly.

The intention of this template is to make sure you, as the author, show the ramifications, and emotional and physical aftermath of the Story Crisis, which happened in the last template. It's also meant to make clear that while there is more story to come, there is a breathing space—an opportunity to acknowledge what has already been lost or gained while making the final decision to continue either toward the External Story Goal or toward a return to the Everyday World to share what's already been earned or learned.

AFTERMATH—REGROUPING/DECISION

The purpose of this template is to show that although change has happened, the character still must make one final push to reach either the External Story Goal or the final step of the Internal Character Growth.

The Character for this template is:

----

1. What internal change has happened to this character as a result of the outcome of Twist Point Two in Chapter 11?

    ----

2. Where is this character physically at this point, and what action is he or she about to take?

    ----

3. What has this character realized as a result of Twist Point Two?

    ----

4. Who else is involved at this point in the story and how?

    ----

5. Has this template character's External Story Goal or part of this goal been met and, if so, how?

    ----

6. What decision does this character make now?

    ----

7. What action happens next?

    ----

1. What internal change has happened to this character as a result of the outcome of Twist Point Two?

   Jason is determined to give himself and Marie a chance at a future together.

2. Where is this character physically at this point, and what action is he or she about to take?

   Jason leaves the farmhouse and returns to Paris to confront the CIA handler who's flown to Paris to make sure Jason is stopped. This sets up an opportunity to track the handler back to a CIA safe house in Paris.

3. What has this character realized as a result of Twist Point Two?

   Even though Jason does not like knowing he was trained as an assassin, he can now use his skills to keep himself alive and take down the CIA handler if necessary.

4. Who else is involved at this point in the story and how?

   Marie because she stands to lose Jason. The CIA handler who assumes he'll come out the winner. The CIA handler's boss who has his own contingency plans in place.

5. Has this template character's External Story Goal or part of this goal been met and, if so, how?

   Yes, Jason knows he was trained as a CIA assassin and is closer to stopping the people who trained him.

6. What decision does this character make now?

   Jason decides to follow the CIA handler back to the safe house and confront him there as a way to free himself of the CIA.

7. What action happens next?

   Jason finds the CIA handler safe house and confronts the handler directly and regains more of his memory in the process.

161

1. **What internal change has happened to this character as a result of the outcome of Twist Point Two?**

   Vivian realizes she doesn't want to be treated as a hooker, particularly by Edward, and is willing to walk away right then until he shows he does care by apologizing, which makes her care more for him in return.

2. **Where is this character physically at this point, and what action is he or she about to take?**

   Edward has asked her for a real date. Edward's ordered jewels for her to wear to make the night more special so she's allowing herself to let go and enjoy the experience. Just as Edward focuses on only Vivian's pleasure for the opera, Vivian later focuses on Edward's enjoyment as they make love and she kisses him on the mouth, a metaphor to show that she's not having sex for money but being intimate, and that she forgives him.

3. **What has this character realized as a result of Twist Point Two?**

   Vivian realizes she loves Edward.

4. **Who else is involved at this point in the story and how?**

   Edward, as her date and lover.

5. **Has this template character's External Story Goal or part of this goal been met and, if so, how?**

   Vivian has earned enough money to pay the rent and have money left over so she's achieved financial security and a way out of prostitution.

6. **What decision does this character make now?**

   Vivian decides to spend the remaining time with Edward simply enjoying him.

7. **What action happens next?**

   When Edward blows off a business meeting, they spend an afternoon in the park and talk late into the night.

1. **What internal change has happened to this character as a result of the outcome of Twist Point Two?**

   When Edward takes Vivian to the opera as an apology, this is something very personal to him—evident by traveling to another city away from the superficial world he lives in. Edward is feeling emotionally connected to Vivian as a result of her enjoyment of the opera and making love later that evening is intimate, rather than business.

2. **Where is this character physically at this point, and what action is he or she about to take?**

   Edward flies her via private jet to the opera where Edward is more focused on Vivian's enjoyment and her reaction than his own reactions. Later when he's driving around and stops at a dive so Vivian can see her roommate, Edward is very protective and possessive of Vivian when thugs approach her. Note: Earlier VHS versions of this movie may not have this scene.

3. **What has this character realized as a result of Twist Point Two?**

   Edward realizes he really cares what Vivian feels, more so than his own feelings. And that he enjoys her pleasure and doesn't want anything bad to happen to her.

4. **Who else is involved at this point in the story and how?**

   Vivian as his real date and not his paid companion.

5. **Has this template character's External Story Goal or part of this goal been met and, if so, how?**

   Yes, Edward decides to change the way he does business. He will not be acquiring the family-owned business to dismantle it, but he will be joining forces with the grandfatherly businessman as a partner.

6. **What decision does this character make now?**

Edward decides to enjoy life more. To be less about work and more about experiencing life, which means walking out of a meeting, blowing off half a business day, and going to the park with Vivian just to spend time with her.

7. **What action happens next?**

His lawyer, who's not happy about Edward's behavior or the business decision Edward made, decides to approach Vivian and punish her when he can't find Edward.

1. **What internal change has happened to this character as a result of the outcome of Twist Point Two?**

    Rick is surprised at Ilsa pulling a gun on him to get the Letters of Transit, then realizes she still cares for him, and is even willing to stay with him, but Rick can't stand to see her harmed.

2. **Where is this character physically at this point, and what action is he or she about to take?**

    Rick and Ilsa are upstairs in his apartment over the bar. Ilsa is telling Rick she still loves him. Rick sends Ilsa home with one of his staff and goes down to see Laszlo who was injured at a resistance meeting that night. When Laszlo asks Rick for the papers just for Ilsa as the police come in, Rick makes a decision to help Ilsa and Laszlo, but tells no one what he's doing.

3. **What has this character realized as a result of Twist Point Two?**

    Rick realizes that he still cares deeply for Ilsa, so much that her freedom and safety mean more to him than keeping her with him. Rick also realizes he's a patriot at heart and must commit to taking the side of the freedom fighters in the war.

4. **Who else is involved at this point in the story and how?**

    Ilsa, because she says she'll stay if Rick will get Laszlo out. Laszlo, who is trying to get Ilsa out before he's taken away. Captain Renault, who will suffer consequences if he fails to get the papers and keep Laszlo from leaving. The German major, who will do anything to stop Laszlo.

5. Has this template character's External Story Goal or part of this goal been met or changed and, if so, how?

In making a decision to help Ilsa and Laszlo escape, which will further the resistance movement, Rick's taken a strong step closer to choosing a side to support in the war.

6. What decision does this character make now?

Rick decides to help Laszlo and Ilsa. But first he appears to set up Laszlo as buying the stolen papers so Captain Renault can arrest him and look good to the Germans. Rick tells Ilsa he has a plan, to just trust him.

7. What action happens next?

When Captain Renault confronts Laszlo to arrest him and Ilsa, Rick turns a gun on him and makes the Captain phone the airport to ensure no one stops him, but the Captain actually dials the German major who is alerted to the escape.

1. **What internal change has happened to this character as a result of the outcome of Twist Point Two?**

   Marlin is feeling a lot more secure about taking risks and handling the bad as well as the good things that happen in life.

2. **Where is this character physically at this point, and what action is he or she about to take?**

   Marlin has reached Sydney and they (he and Dory) have accepted the pelican's help. Marlin flies via the pelican to the dentist's office and discovers Nemo is alive.

3. **What has this character realized as a result of Twist Point Two?**

   Marlin has realized that he has to give life his all for the good things to happen and that there are good individuals in the world who will help him.

4. **Who else is involved at this point in the story and how?**

   Dory because she's staying with Marlin. Nemo because he sees that his dad has come through for him. The pelican and other fish in the dentist's office because they are rooting for Nemo to be reunited with his dad.

5. **Has this template character's External Story Goal or part of this goal been met or changed and, if so, how?**

   Yes, partially met. The goal has been met in that Marlin found Nemo, but now Marlin must save his son.

6. **What decision does this character make now?**

   Marlin decides to trust that the pelican will get Marlin into the dentist's office to save Nemo.

7. **What action happens next?**

   The dentist slams the window shut on them and it looks like Nemo is killed.

13 POWER PLOTTING
Transformation—Twist Point Three

> "All of life is about transformation. We are born, we grow, we change, and we die."
> —Theresa Myers, author of *Salvation of the Damned*

You, as the author, have been driving your story to this point all the way. This is the culmination of all the character's experiences, lessons learned, and insights gained. This is the Climax of your story. If you think of Twist Point Two as scaling the first major mountain then Twist Point Three is striving for the highest summit. The intention of this Twist Point or final test is to confirm to your reader that your protagonist truly has changed as a person and will never go back to what he or she was at the beginning of your story. If this test is nonexistent or played down, a reader will feel the story is incomplete and is missing something vital. And they will be correct.

Think of the movie *The Sixth Sense*. The young boy faced his Twist Point Two in the middle of the story when he went to the gathering of family after a little girl had died. The boy found a box the girl had hid and brought the box to the girl's father with the message that his daughter wanted him to see it. This was frightening for the boy since he was making public the fact he could see dead people. On the other hand, these were strangers. If they didn't believe him, he'd never have to see them again. But because they did believe him, the boy was able to join into his school life in a different way and accept who he was. But he still had to face his Transformation. To do that, he has to tell his mother about his gift. She had been his only constant, his only support, so the risk is enormous for him. But until he tells her, the viewer cannot walk away from the story and believe the little boy will be all right.

Many times a significant External Goal can be reached or completed at Twist Point Two: The castle was stormed and overtaken, the poker game won, the relationship consummated. If this is the case, what remains is to verify that internal change has also happened. In romance novels, this is often where one or both characters must face their obstacles to love—a *belief system* that must change before they can accept love. In a mystery, if it appears as though the killer was captured at Twist Point Two and the threat seems to be over, then at Twist Point Three the sleuth—through facing an internal realization or change—will discover and confront the true killer, one he or she never suspected or wanted to believe was capable of murder.

In *Top Gun*, Maverick (Tom Cruise) faces a situation he has faced twice before. The first time, he was a cocky pilot who thought he was invincible. But he learned he's not invincible because the second time he used the same risky move while flying his plane, he killed his best friend (Chapter 11, Stakes Raised). Now Maverick has an opportunity to use the move again and risks death, or if he doesn't die, he stands to risk the lives of his fellow pilots.

> *Motivation, or knowing why your character acts the way he or she does, is the most important aspect of character development.*
> —Maureen Hardegree, award-winning author whose stories are featured in the Mossy Creek Hometown series

The intention of this template is to make sure this final Twist Point—your Climax, where the protagonist has one last chance to give up or make a Herculean effort of some type—will truly show lessons learned and insights solidified. Another death occurs here—literal, physical, symbolic, etc. That true Transformation and Internal Character Growth has occurred. You'll want to make sure what happens here is tied in with the rest of your story and is not simply another test or obstacle thrown in from left field.

TRANSFORMATION—TWIST POINT THREE

The purpose for this template is to clarify that Internal Character Growth has happened.

The Character for this template is:

----

1. What external action or challenge does this character face at this point?

----

2. How does this external action influence the character's External Story Goal?

----

3. What death happens, and in what form does death occur at this point?

   TIP: This could be literal, physical, metaphorical, etc.

----

4. What internal lesson has been learned or is being learned by this character and how does it relate to the character's overall Internal Character Growth?

----

5. What action Is happening in the story at this point?

----

6. Does this character return to his or her Everyday World? If so, how is he or she different?

----

7. Who else is Impacted and how?

----

1. **What external action or challenge does this character face at this point?**

   Jason is battling the CIA handler at the CIA safe house.

2. **How does this external action influence the character's External Story Goal?**

   This final confrontation unlocks some key memories Jason has blocked about who he was and what he did for the CIA and allows him to make a choice to walk away from Treadstone after dismantling their operation in Paris.

3. **What death happens, and in what form does death occur at this point?**

   The death of illusions; that Jason no longer believes his past must equal his future. It is metaphorical. Jason is also risking physical death.

4. **What internal lesson has been learned or is being learned by this character and how does it relate to the character's overall Internal Character Growth?**

   Jason has learned that the past does not have to repeat itself and does not define his future. That though he was once an assassin he does not have to continue to embrace that career or lifestyle. That he has a chance at a different future, one with Marie.

5. **What action is happening in the story at this point?**

   Jason is preparing to walk away from his old life even if it means having the CIA chasing him.

6. **Does this character return to his or her Everyday World? If so, how is he or she different?**

   Jason returns to the people of his Everyday World—the clandestine, secretive world of the CIA, but because of his realizations and growth and change as a character, he no longer chooses to belong to that world.

7. **Who else is impacted and how?**

The CIA handler, who still is making plans to continue to hunt down and eliminate Jason. The CIA handler's boss, who's covering his own position. Marie, who is trusting that if Jason lives they can have a life together.

1. **What external action or challenge does this character face at this point?**

    Vivian is preparing to leave Edward after he offers her a paid arrangement long-term and not a real relationship.

2. **How does this external action influence the character's External Story Goal?**

    Vivian has achieved her external goal of financial security because she's earned her money for being a companion for the week and in so doing now is confident enough to pursue a different way of life.

3. **What death happens, and in what form does death occur at this point?**

    The death of Vivian's relationship with Edward when he can offer her no more than being a kept mistress.

4. **What internal lesson has been learned or is being learned by this character and how does it relate to the character's overall Internal Character Growth?**

    Vivian has learned she is more than her occupation. Vivian's Internal Character Growth was about self-worth, and this goal is achieved.

5. **What action is happening in the story at this point?**

    Vivian is walking away from Edward after declining his offer of being his kept mistress.

6. **Does this character return to his or her Everyday World? If so, how is he or she different?**

    Vivian returns to where she'd been a hooker, but she's dressed differently and she's more secure in herself. She is planning to start a new occupation.

7. **Who else is impacted and how?**

    Edward and her roommate. Edward, because he stands to lose Vivian forever and her roommate because Vivian shares enough money to help the roommate step away from being a prostitute and attend beauty school.

1. **What external action or challenge does this character face at this point?**
Edward gives Vivian a choice—the same choice he's given to all his previous girlfriends—stay with him on his terms. Vivian does not accept his terms. This in turn leads to a separation.

2. **How does this external action influence the character's External Story Goal?**
Edward has achieved his external goal of acquiring a company and changing how he does business. Vivian's staying or not staying does not impact this goal, although her presence helped him make the transition.

3. **What death happens, and in what form does death occur at this point?**
The death of Edward's relationship with Vivian. Metaphorical death.

4. **What internal lesson has been learned or is being learned by this character and how does it relate to the character's overall Internal Character Growth?**
Edward learns that money is not always enough. That he's only been willing to give money in the past, never risking giving of himself. He's learning that, for the right woman, there's a lot more to give and receive. Edward's Internal Character Growth was to learn how to connect emotionally with other people. While he has connected emotionally, he is still denying a simple truth—that to receive he must be willing to give. That to have a true relationship with a woman he has to go out on a limb and risk exposing his true feelings.

5. **What action is happening in the story at this point?**
Edward is preparing to leave Hollywood and return to New York.

6. **Does this character return to his or her Everyday World? If so, how is he or she different?**

   Edward has never left his Everyday World, but now he experiences it differently in that he no longer shuts people out. Thus when the hotel manager mentions that the driver of the limo knows where Vivian lives, Edward is able to hear him and even recalls the manager's name.

7. **Who else is impacted and how?**

   Vivian, because even though she's in love with Edward, she has the confidence now to stand on her own two feet and to accept nothing less than love and respect.

1. **What external action or challenge does this character face at this point?**

   Rick is holding a gun on Captain Renault at the airport as Ilsa and Laszlo flee on the airplane and the German major is coming.

2. **How does this external action influence the character's External Story Goal?**

   This ends the External Story Goal because Rick has taken a side.

3. **What death happens, and in what form does death occur at this point?**

   For Rick, the death is metaphorical in that his illusion that he can remain neutral dies. He also faces physical death if his plans to use the Letters of Transit backfire.

4. **What internal lesson has been learned or is being learned by this character and how does it relate to the character's overall Internal Character Growth?**

   That Rick cannot sit on the sideline without a cost. That love and the emotional pain it brings also brings connection, something he's been missing since Paris. Rick's Internal Character Growth was to thaw his heart so he could connect with others, which happens as he realizes that to receive love he has to give love. He does this when he puts Ilsa and her husband's needs before his own.

5. **What action is happening in the story at this point?**

   Rick's neutrality is changing. He's putting into effect a series of steps that will make him actively resisting the Germans.

6. **Does this character return to his or her Everyday World? If so, how is he or she different?**

   Rick has sold his café and thus cut his ties with having to stay in Casablanca, so he's making plans to leave his Everyday World with the French captain. And by making an anti-German choice, he's firmly declared which side of the war he supports.

7. **Who else is impacted and how?**

   Ilsa, by admitting that she still loves Rick and expects to stay with him in Casablanca. Her husband, who's willing to die alone and send her off with another man rather than risk her life. The French captain, who becomes an unwitting pawn in Rick's plans. The German major, who thinks he'll be able to stop Laszlo and punish Rick for his part in letting Laszlo escape.

1. **What external action or challenge does this character face at this point?**

   Nemo has freed himself from the dentist's office and finds Marlin, but Dory becomes caught up in the commercial fishing net. Marlin faces having to rescue or abandon her.

2. **How does this external action influence the character's External Story Goal?**

   Marlin has been reunited with his son, but stands to lose Dory if they turn their backs on her. If he chooses to saves her, then he has broadened his definition as a father by showing his son how to care about others.

3. **What death happens, and in what form does death occur at this point?**

   For all the fish in the net, including Dory, they stand to face a literal death. For Marlin to choose a different action when encountering danger—to face it instead of running or hiding from it—means a metaphorical death of an old habit, old fears, and old patterns.

4. **What internal lesson has been learned or is being learned by this character and how does it relate to the character's overall Internal Character Growth?**

   Marlin is learning that he can face his fears and make a change. He can work with Nemo instead of assuming Nemo needs his protection. Marlin's Internal Character Growth was to learn to let go of overprotecting Nemo and to expand his parental vision, which he's able to do at last.

5. **What action is happening in the story at this point?**

   Marlin and Nemo are able to save all the fish, including Dory, so Marlin is able to face the world unafraid. As a result he can let Nemo act independently and start to live life instead of cowering from it.

6. **Does this character return to his or her Everyday World? If so, how is he or she different?**

   Yes, Marlin and Nemo return home; only now Marlin is able to be excited about the day instead of anxious. He's able to let Nemo go off on an adventure with his school buddies.

7. **Who else is impacted and how?**

   Nemo, because now his dad is engaged in life. Dory, because she belongs to Marlin's world. Marlin's fish neighbors because now Marlin is an active part of the community.

14 POWER PLOTTING
Wins and Losses—Lessons Learned and Shared

" If we don't share our lessons, we are bound to repeat our mistakes. "
—Kathleen R. Jorgensen, author of *Man's Best Friend*

At this final phase in your story you'll want to make sure two major issues are covered. The first is that you have resolved all outstanding story questions and tied up all plot lines. The second is that it's clear that your protagonist and possibly other characters in some way use the lessons learned and shared with the larger community.

This is to show that what they have learned, encountered, and experienced has served a purpose. With American fiction in particular, one of the most common ways this is done is by having your character return to his or her Everyday World, but he or she does not return as he or she was at the beginning of your story but, forever changed. Even if your character does not return to the Everyday World, still bring in an opportunity to show the reader that the character has changed and will not revert to previous actions or behaviors.

In a mystery series, where you don't necessarily want huge character change to happen to the protagonist between novels, one way to show Lessons Learned and Shared is to show the addition of a new friend or relationship the sleuth has made as a result of the story. Even the promise of such will give the "community benefit" feel to your story. In romance novels, one of the ways the returning to community happens is through a wedding scene or the impending arrival of a new child. Both show that others share in the love, or that through love the family unit is strengthened and continued.

In *Notting Hill,* this area of the story is when William Thacker first talks with his community of friends about Anna bringing him a priceless painting and his turning down her offer to get together again—Wins and Losses. Then he goes after Anna Scott at the press conference. His proposal and her acceptance are witnessed not only by friends but by the world press, thus sharing joy with many—Lessons Learned and Shared. They are also married, where family and friends from two different worlds are brought together to benefit and lastly, both characters are seen enjoying one another's worlds as well as preparing to bring a child into the world from their union. In *Bridget Jones's Diary* this is where Mark Darcy returns to Bridget, creating the External Story Goal she wanted—a relationship with a good man.

One more element of this area in your story is to set up the next story if you are writing a series. In the last pages you bring out the secondary character or story line more strongly for the next book if you have a returning protagonist—hook the reader into questions raised and not answered in these last pages about that character or story line and you'll have built in a need for the reader to look for your next release.

The intention of this template is to resolve all outstanding story questions, make sure that issues from External Story Goal and Internal Character Growth raised at the beginning of your story or elsewhere are resolved and explained. You also have the opportunity to set up future books or story lines by either bringing in secondary characters in a larger way or story questions threaded in to hook the reader for the next book in the series. And the key element here is to reassure and confirm for the reader that all the struggles, losses, pain, and lessons benefit not only your protagonist, but the larger community. This ensures the reader receives the payoff expected for having invested the time in your story.

WINS AND LOSSES—LESSONS LEARNED AND SHARED

The purpose for this template is to resolve all outstanding story questions.

The Character for this template is:

----

1. As a result of the Transformation (Chapter 13), what has happened to this character?

    ----

2. What external reward, if any, has this character achieved at this point in his or her story?

    ----

3. What internal lesson has this character learned as a result of the Climax or Twist Point Three (especially if he or she had not learned the lesson before that section of the story)?

    ----

4. Who else is impacted by the character learning his or her internal lesson and reaching the final stage of his or her Internal Character Growth and how?

    ----

5. Does the character return to his or her Everyday World? Why or why not and what has changed for him or her?

    ----

6. How does this compare to where this character started the story?

MOVIE EXAMPLE:
The Bourne Identity

THE CHARACTER FOR THIS TEMPLATE IS:
Jason Bourne (Matt Damon)

1. **As a result of the Transformation, what has happened to this character?**

   Jason accepts that in spite of his past career that he is more than his prior actions. As the result of making different choices in the future, he can have a different kind of life, starting with a relationship with a woman who cares for him.

2. **What external reward, if any, has this character achieved at this point in his or her story?**

   Jason is able to walk away from the CIA and reunite with Marie.

3. **What internal lesson has this character learned as a result of the Climax or Twist Point Three (especially if he or she had not learned the lesson by that section of the story)?**

   Jason has learned that he's more than his past memories. His original goal was an assumption that if he found out who he was then his world would make sense. Now he realizes that what he did before is not who he is today, and that in order to be an integrated, whole person he needs to make some changes in his life, beginning with greater connection, starting with Marie.

4. **Who else is impacted by the character learning his or her internal lesson and reaching the final stage of his or her Internal Character Growth and how?**

   Marie, because he finds her and wants to be with her. The CIA handler's boss, as he continues to cover up the secret operation that Jason was a part of, thus continuing the lies and setting up story lines for the next story in the series.

5. Does the character return to his or her Everyday World? Why or why not, and what is different for this character now in his or her Everyday World if they returned?

No, Jason walks away from his Everyday World of being a covert CIA assassin. Jason is connected with a woman who can know who he really is. He's no longer an assassin. He's free to make different choices about his future.

6. How does this compare to where this character started the story?

At the beginning of the story, Jason was a man without a past who thought knowing that past would anchor him to the present and allow him a future. Instead his past threatened to destroy any possibility of a future. But rather than running from that past, he confronted it, which has now given him a fresh start.

1. **As a result of the Transformation, what has happened to this character?**
    Vivian returns to her Everyday World and sets about building a new life for her roommate and for herself without Edward, when he comes and offers his love to her.

2. **What external reward, if any, has this character achieved at this point in his or her story?**
    The implied security of knowing Vivian has what it takes internally to stand on her own without sacrificing her self respect and that in doing so she can achieve her dreams. She also has a great new wardrobe and enough funds to allow both herself and her roommate to quit being prostitutes.

3. **What internal lesson has this character learned as a result of the Climax or Twist Point Three (especially if he or she had not learned the lesson by that section of the story)?**
    Because Vivian accepts that she is more than what she did as a hooker, she can accept and think of herself as a worthy person. She has self-worth vs. defining herself based on other people's perceptions.

4. **Who else is impacted by the character learning his or her internal lesson and reaching the final stage of his or her Internal Character Growth and how?**
    Edward, because when he charges up to "save" her, Vivian meets him halfway. In doing so, she accepts the implied offer of marriage, because her decision and actions are now driven from a place of security vs. a place of vulnerability, want, or necessity.

5. **Does the character return to his or her Everyday World? Why or why not, and what is different for this character now in his or her Everyday World if they returned?**

    Yes, Vivian returned, but everything is different. She is dressed differently. She feels differently about herself. She is able to encourage her roommate to consider an alternative life, plus Vivian is facing the future with different expectations.

6. **How does this compare to where this character started the story?**

    Vivian started the story living hand to mouth and being defined by her job. Now she's defining herself by her goals and her aspirations. She started the story with friends, but was valued only for her sexual expertise and not loved. Now she has Edward, who values her as an equal and loves her.

1. As a result of the Transformation, what has happened to this character?

   Edward realizes how alone and isolated he really is because of his choices and decisions. That being the king in the castle is not enough and that there is more to life than material things.

2. What external reward, if any, has this character achieved at this point in his or her story?

   Edward has achieved a new direction in his business, from dismantling and destroying to building and growing. This gives a larger meaning to what he does daily. He's also earned Vivian's love.

3. What internal lesson has this character learned as a result of the Climax or Twist Point Three (especially if he or she had not learned the lesson by that section of the story)?

   Edward has learned to take emotional risks in order to connect with another. Yes, this meets his original internal need to get in touch with his emotions and connect.

4. Who else is impacted by the character learning his or her internal lesson and reaching the final stage of his or her Internal Character Growth and how?

   Vivian, because now Edward is truly able to offer her his love and not just his money.

5. Does the character return to his or her Everyday World? Why or why not, and what is different for this character now in his or her Everyday World if they returned?

   Edward never left it, but perceives his Everyday World differently now. He's aware of the people in his Everyday World and he's willing to leave that world long enough to go after Vivian in hers.

continued

6. **How does this compare to where this character started the story?**

    Edward is emotionally connected at the end of the
    story where he wasn't at the beginning. He's willing
    to face his fear of heights to prove his commitment
    to Vivian which he never would have done at the
    beginning. He's got a whole new direction to his
    business and has jettisoned his jerk of a lawyer. And
    he now has the love of his life—Vivian.

WINS AND LOSSES—LESSONS LEARNED AND SHARED
MOVIE EXAMPLE:
Casablanca

THE CHARACTER FOR THIS TEMPLATE IS:
Richard "Rick" Blaine (Humphrey Bogart)

1. As a result of the Transformation, what has happened to this character?

Rick's no longer emotionally distant from life and the people in his world.

2. What external reward, if any, has this character achieved at this point in his or her story?

Rick's reward is to be able to not only help Ilsa who has admitted her love for him but to help a larger cause by getting her husband to freedom where he can continue his work to stop the Germans and continue to bring hope to those under German oppression.

3. What internal lesson has this character learned as a result of the Climax or Twist Point Three (especially if he or she had not learned the lesson by that section of the story)?

Rick has learned that to feel is to be alive. When he shut off his emotions, he was existing but not living. With Ilsa's coming back into his life, Rick is able to re-engage with his emotions and thus engage with life.

4. Who else is impacted by the character learning his or her internal lesson and reaching the final stage of his or her Internal Character Growth and how?

Ilsa and her husband, because they are free to go to America and continue working for the resistance movement. The French Captain Renault, who has also faced his own complacency and will now be leaving with Rick. The German major, who died because he was inflexible.

5. **Does the character return to his or her Everyday World? Why or why not, and what is different for this character now in his or her Everyday World if they returned?**

    No. Rick sold his bar and planned to leave his Everyday World before helping Ilsa and Laszlo escape. While Rick is still in North Africa, he is not returning to being the isolated, unemotional café owner. He's thrown in his lot with the side of the free French and against the Germans so he'll be leaving shortly to find a new place to live, so that he can continue to fight against the Germans.

6. **How does this compare to where this character started the story?**

    Rick has become re-engaged in life, willing to once again fight for the underdog. His emotions are no longer frozen. He's learned to sacrifice without any hope of a reward and knows the love of his life will be safe and out of harm's way. This is a total change from where he was at the beginning of the story.

1. As a result of the Transformation, what has happened to this character?

Marlin has learned to live life fully and to have a strong, healthy non-codependent relationship with his son.

2. What external reward, if any, has this character achieved at this point in his or her story?

Marlin has achieved the renewed love of his son and a place in the community of fish.

3. What internal lesson has this character learned as a result of the Climax or Twist Point Three (especially if he or she had not learned the lesson by that section of the story)?

Marlin regained his sense of security in the world. He's now able to allow his son to experience life, which Nemo was unable to do before because of Marlin's fears.

4. Who else is impacted by the character learning his or her internal lesson and reaching the final stage of his or her Internal Character Growth and how?

Nemo, because now his dad Marlin is engaged in life and sharing that engagement with Nemo. Dory, who has found a new community of fish to belong to as well as her continued friendship with Marlin. The community of fish, because Marlin is now interactive with them rather than reclusive.

5. Does the character return to his or her Everyday World? Why or why not, and what is different for this character now in his or her Everyday World if they returned?

   Yes, Marlin has returned, but now perceives his world differently. Marlin is excited to start every day rather than fearful. He's part of a larger community rather than isolated. He's able to allow Nemo to live a larger life rather than constantly protecting him, expanding Marlin's conception of being a good father.

6. How does this compare to where this character started the story?

   Marlin is prodding Nemo to get to school as opposed to trying to keep him at home.

Part III
DON'T LET THEM PUT THE BOOK DOWN

Power Pacing: Forward—Quickly . . . or Not
Powerful Endings: Make Them Want More
Dialogue: It's More Than Talking Heads
The Final Stage of Writing

What held your attention the last time you stayed awake all night reading a book? Pacing.

That word is batted around when writers meet to discuss their books. Great pacing is at the core of all wonderful books that readers tell other readers about who then tell more readers. Every author wants to hear a reader say, "I couldn't put it down." As a writer, it is your job to make it difficult for a reader to put that book down no matter what.

Part of great pacing is wonderful dialogue, which we've included as a bonus in this book. Let someone else read your dialogue out loud to hear how the unfamiliar reader experiences the conversations between characters. Too often, as authors, we hear the whole conversation in our head between the characters and *know* how it sounds. It's important to hear how a cold reader interprets the dialogue.

The big payoff of your story is The End. If the beginning sells your first book, the ending sells your next one. Readers want an ending that makes them cheer for the protagonist who fought hard and long to reach his or her goal. Make sure you give readers maximum payoff in the end and they'll be back for more.

15 POWER PACING
Forward—Quickly . . . or Not

"The best way to be boring is to leave nothing out."

—Voltaire

There are a million reasons a reader can set a book down. And a reader needs only one reason to pick the book up again. The desire or curiosity to learn what is going to happen next is what drives readers to continue reading or pick up the book again after their schedule has *forced* them to put it down.

This is called "pacing." If a reader *cannot* abandon your book until they find out what happens to your characters you've created great pacing. Notice something very important in that statement—"what happens to your characters" The goal is to make a personal connection between reader and character, to make this reader care about whatever your character is facing.

If a reader (editor) can't put your book down you increase your chances of selling your manuscript.

Great pacing is not simply a roller-coaster ride whipping through a book—though that can be one element of pacing. So don't confuse a plot heavy with action with a fast-paced plot.

One hundred years ago, a novelist was not required to grip and hold captive a reader's attention. Twenty years ago, a compelling yarn well plotted was enough to hold the average reader. Today we're competing against television, movies, iPods, and schedules already overloaded and stretched to the breaking point. We're asking two things of our readers—invest your money and invest your time—every time they pick up one of our books.

And of the two, time is often the more precious commodity.

Pacing is not relentless wringer scenes or lurching from potential death to potential death. It is more about an emotionally satisfying read that doesn't exhaust your reader in the process. Every element of your story is involved in pacing—your opening page, each chapter, each scene, and each word as well as the book as a whole.

> *The one thing that will kill pacing is not having a concrete story goal for even one scene in your book.*
>
> —Joanne Rock, award-winning author of *A Knight Most Wicked*

Pacing means understanding when you should slow readers down to catch their breath or speed them up to turn those pages. But even when you slow things down, pacing is not sacrificed. The story must continue to move forward. You can't stop for a chat in a diner unless that chat plays a powerful role in the story's development.

Let's face it—readers know, before they even open your book, what the ultimate outcome is going to be if you write commercial fiction. They are guaranteed that the hero and heroine will get together for a HEA (Happily Ever After) if they are reading a romance; that the killer will be brought to justice if they are reading a mystery; that the world or species will be saved if they are reading a sci-fi story.

Pacing is not the destination but how you get your readers there.

Speed is not the only issue to consider in pacing—variation is as important. Keep the following list in mind to vary pacing.

To Create Faster Pacing Use:

Shorter chapters
More dialogue
Very little narrative or description
Action instead of tags in dialogue

Sexual tension

Ticking clock = something must happen soon

Two or more characters on scene

Subplots echoing the main plot

Shorter sentences

New questions

To Slow Pacing (and still keep scene active) Use:

More internal dialogue

More narrative

More description

Longer chapters with longer reaction/decision scenes

One character per scene

Longer sentences

Characters having sex

To Flat-Line Pacing Use:

Vague details

Repetitive information

Dialogue about banalities ("Hi, how are you?" "I am fine. And you?" "I am fine.")

A shift in focus from the main story to a secondary story or character

Little risk or no conflict

Back story given in large chunks

No change in an action/disaster scene or in a chapter

Characters who only react and never act

Heavy internal dialogue

POWER PLOTTING TIP Keep in mind genre differences—what's fast pacing in a work of women's fiction is not fast in a thriller. Use the template to analyze scenes within the genre you are writing. Use the template to analyze the difference between the opening scene in a story, before the climax, after the climax, and in between in stories you enjoy as there should be differences. Soon you'll start to see and understand pacing better and translate that pacing to your own story.

POWER PACING TEMPLATE

The purpose of this template is to determine if each scene has a goal and conflict, if the characters are moving with a purpose, and if the scene moves the story forward.

Scene selection for this template is:

POV character for this scene is:

----

1. What is the reason this scene *must* be in this (character)'s POV?

----

2. What is the POV character's Immediate External Goal in this scene?

----

3. What major action/development will occur in this scene and how will that impact the plot?

----

4. How will the aftermath of the above action/development impact the character internally?

----

5. What is creating the urgency in this scene?

    ----

6. By the end of this scene, the plot will have changed and moved
    forward how?

    ----

1. **What is the reason this scene *must* be in this character's POV?**

   It's in Jason's POV, because he has the most to lose if he does not convince Marie to accept his offer of a financial bargain to help him. Due to amnesia, he doesn't know anyone else to ask for help.

2. **What is the POV character's Immediate External Goal in this scene?**

   Jason's most immediate goal is to escape Zurich and get to Paris.

3. **What major action/development will occur in this scene and how will that impact the plot?**

   Teaming up with Marie creates an ally for Jason. By allowing her to help him, he puts both of them at risk.

4. **How will the aftermath of the above action/development impact the character internally?**

   Jason must extend some trust to even make a deal with someone (Marie).

5. **What is creating the urgency in this scene?**

   The sooner Jason gets to Paris, the sooner he'll find more answers.

6. **By the end of this scene, the plot will have changed and moved forward how?**

   Instead of answers in Paris, Jason will find more questions plus now Marie's life is in danger, too.

1. **What is the reason this scene *must* be in this character's POV?**

   This is Vivian's scene. She has just realized she doesn't have money to make the rent payment, so she must convince Edward to make a deal.

2. **What is the POV character's Immediate External Goal in this scene?**

   Vivian's immediate goal is to make a deal to earn money for rent.

3. **What major action/development will occur in this scene and how will that impact the plot?**

   Vivian will meet Edward and, for a fee, will get into his car and direct him to his hotel, which impacts the plot by putting her in the position of at least asking him to pay for sex.

4. **How will the aftermath of the above action/development impact the character internally?**

   Being in Edward's world, Vivian feels out of her element, but she is willing to fight to stay.

5. **What is creating the urgency in this scene?**

   The urgency driving this scene is Vivian's desperation to make the rent money.

6. **By the end of this scene, the plot will have changed and moved forward how?**

   The plot will have changed from Vivian only trying to get partial rent money to Vivian agreeing to stay in Edward's world longer and thus earn more money.

Casablanca

SCENE SELECTION FOR THIS TEMPLATE IS:
First scene in Rick's Café

POV CHARACTER FOR THIS SCENE IS:
Richard "Rick" Blaine (Humphrey Bogart)

1. **What is the reason this scene *must* be in this character's POV?**

   It's in Rick's POV because this is his story and we see what is at stake with hiding the Letters of Transit.

2. **What is the POV character's Immediate External Goal in this scene?**

   Rick's initial goal is to not get involved in the emotions and drama around him, which includes taking a side in the war.

3. **What major action/development will occur in this scene and how will that impact the plot?**

   Rick will come into possession of stolen Letters of Transit and his former love—Ilsa Lund—will re-enter his life. These two events will force Rick to get in touch with his emotions and eventually choose to take a side in the war.

4. **How will the aftermath of the above action/development impact the character internally?**

   Where Rick was prepared not to act on using the Letters of Transit, once Ilsa enters his life again, he'll begin to have second thoughts about not using the documents.

5. **What is creating the urgency in this scene?**

   The urgency in the scene is driven by the thief who stole the documents being captured and Ilsa showing up, which creates a dilemma for Rick as to what to do with documents.

6. **By the end of this scene, the plot will have changed and moved forward how?**

By the end of the scene, the plot moves forward by starting Rick on a path of reconnecting (by going from being so alone he plays chess alone to sharing drinks with Ilsa and Laszlo). Note: Compared to a scene geared toward a more contemporary audience this scene is quite slow, because there are several repeated sequences—people talking about Rick and to Rick, noting how he is uninvolved—before the disaster of Ilsa's arrival. Notice how repetition slows a scene rather than speeds it up.

1. **What is the reason this scene *must* be in this character's POV?**

    This must be in Marlin's POV. This is his story and it starts with the loss of his family.

2. **What is the POV character's Immediate External Goal in this scene?**

    Marlin's initial external goal is to make sure his wife is happy and that he's done everything possible to create a perfect place to raise their family.

3. **What major action/development will occur in this scene and how will that impact the plot?**

    A predator fish attacks Marlin's wife, as Marlin swims toward her to protect her (which shows that at one time Marlin was not afraid and could act instead of cowering from life), but his entire family is killed except for one egg (one child).

4. **How will the aftermath of the above action/development impact the character internally?**

    This tragedy sets up Marlin's internal fears and motivation to not let his son Nemo move beyond the safety of their sea anemone.

5. **What is creating the urgency in this scene?**

    The urgency is that Marlin's family is being attacked.

6. **By the end of this scene, the plot will have changed and moved forward how?**

    Now Marlin will have strong motivation to protect his remaining child, Nemo, at all costs.

16 POWERFUL ENDINGS
Make Them Want More

> " Great is the art of beginning, but greater is the art of ending. "
>
> —Longfellow

There is a saying in publishing that the opening sells your first story, but the ending brings them back for your next one.

Every writer approaches a book differently, so you may not know your ending when you start. However, at some point you have to tie up all the loose ends and give the story a solid resolution. In commercial fiction, readers want to know the good guys won, the bad guys were punished, and the world is a better place for what has transpired. Even in a series, the main plot has to be resolved or the reader will feel very disappointed after investing time and emotion with your characters.

Consider the path you're sending your main character on and what the payoff will be for him or her in the end. The reader wants to experience that moment of triumph with the character.

In *The Wizard of Oz*, we're happy to see Dorothy return home where her world is a better place. At the end of *Four Weddings and a Funeral*, we need to know that the main characters Charles (Hugh Grant) and Carrie (Andie McDowell) not only married, but were happy with a child, as well as knowing the other story characters found someone to love and marry. In the sci-fi movie *The Fifth Element*, it's important to not only know that the world was saved from a fiery meteor at the last second, but that Leeloo (Milla Jovovich) and Korben Dallas (Bruce Willis) earn a relationship together after all their efforts.

> *A truly great ending manages to be both inevitable yet surprising. It's exactly what the reader wants, yet she cannot see it coming, or at least, she cannot wait to discover how it will play out.*
>
> —Susan Wiggs, *New York Times* best-selling author

Dynamic endings depend on the significance of a character's External Story Goal (the one you as the writer choose) and the character's motivation to reach that goal. The greater the motivation and more difficult the task, the more we cheer when the character overcomes all obstacles to reach that goal.

The protagonist must reach the final stage of his or her Internal Character Growth and External Story Goal before the story ends and before the epilogue.

POWER PLOTTING TIP In some genres the External Story Goal is resolved before the Internal Character Growth: for example, in romance and women's fiction. In other genres, sometimes the protagonist's Internal Character Growth happens first and allows that character to make the supreme effort to reach the External Story Goal. The endings of movies and books we remember are those where we cheered for the protagonist who sacrificed all to save the world or triumphed over evil or reached a goal after struggling against all odds. Don't cheat your reader or audience with a tepid ending.

POWERFUL ENDINGS TEMPLATE

The purpose of this template is to resolve the end of your story with a strong ending.

The Character for this template is:

----

1. What does this character want externally as he or she approaches the climax (the last huge push to either achieve the External Story Goal or their Internal Character Growth) and how is this in conflict with his or her internal feelings?

   TIP: Start setting up your ending or resolution much earlier than the last few pages of the book.

   ----

2. Why are the stakes high at this point if the character does not reach his or her goal?

   ----

3. What is the climactic moment for this character and what happens?

   ----

4. Give an example of how the character has changed internally since the beginning of the story.

   ----

5. Why will the reader cheer for the character at this moment?

   TIP: This should be the biggest emotional point of the story.

   ----

6. How are any Secondary Story Lines or Subplots resolved?

   ----

7. What is the emotional feel of the end of the story? Why?

   ----

1. **What does this character want externally as he or she approaches the climax and how is this in conflict with his or her internal feelings?**

   Jason's main external goal late in the story is to find Treadstone Headquarters to determine if there is a way to be free of them.

2. **Why are the stakes high at this point if the character does not reach his or her goal?**

   The stakes are high: If Jason doesn't succeed, the CIA will kill him and possibly find and kill Marie.

3. **What is the climactic moment for this character and what happens?**

   All hope is lost when Jason has a final battle at the headquarters of Treadstone outmanned four to one.

4. **Why will the reader cheer for the character at this moment?**

   The reader will cheer because Jason is willing to face the villains head on and survives against all odds to walk away to a future of his own making.

5. **Give an example of how the character has changed internally since the beginning of the story.**

   While Jason still does not know all of his past, he's accepted that his past does not have to be his future. As a result, he's able to trust and connect with Marie—a first for him.

6. **How are any Secondary Story Lines or Subplots resolved?**

   The Subplot was resolved when the more powerful CIA guy had the head of Treadstone assassinated, thereby shutting down Treadstone.

7. **What is the emotional feel of the end of the story? Why?**

   The emotional feel is one of relief because Jason has closed his door on working for the CIA. Also because he makes the effort to find Marie, which gives hope that he's found connection and trust.

Pretty Woman

THE CHARACTER FOR THIS TEMPLATE IS:
Vivian Ward (Julia Roberts)

1. **What does this character want externally as he or she approaches the climax and how is this in conflict with his or her internal feelings?**

    Vivian wants to stay in Edward's world and share a life with him (the key about ending a romance is: Will the couple find a way for happily ever after?), but internally she can no longer accept their relationship as a business deal, which is what his offer to set her up in an apartment amounts to.

2. **Why are the stakes high at this point if the character does not reach his or her goal?**

    Since Vivian has fallen in love with Edward, she stands to lose the one man she knows is worthy of her love.

3. **What is the climactic moment for this character and what happens?**

    The climax is when Edward offers Vivian an arrangement as a mistress. Even though Vivian loves him, she can't remain under those terms and respect herself as a person so she turns him down.

4. **Why will the reader cheer for the character at this moment?**

    The reader cheers for any woman who is not willing to accept second best and will hold out for her true dream.

5. **Give an example of how the character has changed internally since the beginning of the story.**

    Vivian walks away from guaranteed security and a man she knows cares deeply for her, which shows her sense of self-worth has increased dramatically. In the beginning she'd have jumped at his offer.

6. **How are any Secondary Story Lines or Subplots resolved?**

   The roommate-at-risk Secondary Story Line is resolved by Vivian giving her roommate enough money to pay rent and to start beauty school so her roommate can also leave prostitution.

7. **What is the emotional feel of the end of the story? Why?**

   The emotional feel is happy. Edward comes for Vivian because he loves her, which confirms that she is worth his love and more.

Pretty Woman

THE CHARACTER FOR THIS TEMPLATE IS:
Edward Lewis (Richard Gere)

1. **What does this character want externally as he or she approaches the climax and how is this in conflict with his or her internal feelings?**

   Edward's external goal after settling the shipping business deal is to set up Vivian in an apartment as his mistress. He cares for her, but isn't capable of making a personal commitment so he convinces himself he's doing the best he can by offering her security, when in truth it's a safe way to remain emotionally uncommitted.

2. **Why are the stakes high at this point if the character does not reach his or her goal?**

   If Edward does not convince Vivian to accept his offer, he stands to lose the one thing he can't buy or negotiate—Vivian's love.

3. **What is the climactic moment for this character and what happens?**

   Edward realizes all is lost when Vivian turns down his offer to be his mistress.

4. **Why will the reader cheer for the character at this moment?**

   Because Edward rides up to Vivian's apartment building in a white limo (the white charger) with his umbrella drawn as a hero would wield his sword, then faces his worst fear—heights—to climb up the ladder to her where she welcomes him.

5. **Give an example of how the character has changed internally since the beginning of the story.**

   In the beginning, Edward is unable to commit to an emotional arrangement with anyone. By the end, he's willing to make an emotional commitment rather than let the woman he loves walk away.

continued

6. **How are any Secondary Story Lines or Subplots resolved?**

   The Subplot is resolved when Edward forgoes the corporate takeover to form a partnership with the elderly business owner to save the shipping firm.

7. **What is the emotional feel of the end of the story? Why?**

   The emotional feel is happy, because Edward goes after his true love and reaches Vivian before she leaves.

Casablanca

THE CHARACTER FOR THIS TEMPLATE IS:
Richard "Rick" Blaine (Humphrey Bogart)

1. **What does this character want externally as he or she approaches the climax and how is this in conflict with his or her internal feelings?**

   Rick's external goal late in the story is to find a way to help Ilsa and Laszlo get away. The conflict internally for him is that he still loves Ilsa.

2. **Why are the stakes high at this point if the character does not reach his or her goal?**

   If Rick screws up, Ilsa and Laszlo face either being thrown into a concentration camp or killed.

3. **What is the climactic moment for this character and what happens?**

   When Major Strasser shows up at the airport, Rick has no choice but to kill him. Then Renault has only two choices—to either shoot or arrest Rick.

4. **Why will the reader cheer for the character at this moment?**

   The reader cheers for Rick, because he shows selfless love by helping Ilsa and Laszlo escape. Then, Rick rejoins the human race by taking a side in the war.

5. **Give an example of how the character has changed internally since the beginning of the story.**

   At the beginning of the story, Rick was politically neutral and a cynical loner. By the end, Rick has chosen a side in the war because he has opened his heart to Ilsa again. Then he leaves with Renault (the assumption is that Rick returns to freedom fighting).

6. **How are any Secondary Story Lines or Subplots resolved?**

   The Subplot of Ilsa's and Rick's relationship is resolved when he makes her get on the plane with Laszlo.

7. **What is the emotional feel of the end of the story? Why?**

   The emotional feel at the end is a little sad because Rick loses Ilsa, but the stronger emotional feeling is a sense of regained life and purpose for Rick.

1. **What does this character want externally as he or she approaches the climax and how is this in conflict with his or her internal feelings?**

   Marlin wants to return home with Nemo, but Dory is caught in a fishing net. Marlin must put himself and Nemo at risk to save her.

2. **Why are the stakes high at this point if the character does not reach his or her goal?**

   The stakes are high because Marlin will lose Dory and jeopardize his son's safety.

3. **What is the climactic moment for this character and what happens?**

   All hope is lost when Dory is caught in a fishing net, and Marlin realizes he must put himself and his son at risk to save her.

4. **Why will the reader cheer for the character at this moment?**

   We cheer for an individual who has had to face his worst fears to help another, when it would be easier to do nothing.

5. **Give an example of how the character has changed internally since the beginning of the story.**

   Marlin now allows Nemo to swim and live in the larger ocean. Marlin is no longer an overprotective parent, but one who realizes that bad and good things can happen and that risk is a part of a full life.

6. **How are any Secondary Story Lines or Subplots resolved?**

   The Secondary Story Line of the fish in the dentist office aquarium ends when Nemo escapes.

7. **What is the emotional feel of the end of the story? Why?**

   The emotional feel at the end of the story is joy, because both Marlin and Nemo are more fully engaged with life.

17 DIALOGUE
It's More Than Talking Heads

"I researched every milieu. If I were to do a movie
tomorrow about a fashion designer, say, I would have
to spend some time to find out what language they
spoke. Because I would never be satisfied with my
dialogue, I want something that gives you the color of
that character right away."

—Samuel Fuller, director and screenwriter of
Pickup on South Street and *White Dog*

Dialogue, defined as conversation or an exchange of words, needs to be
both realistic and nonrealistic. First, let's talk about the nonrealistic.
The reason you get what's called "sound bites" on television from an
interview is that most people would not sit through all the boring dialogue. If you don't have a really good reason for dialogue, it's boring to
the reader. They aren't interested in listening in on a mundane conversation that shares no juicy gossip. They want to hear the scoop.

Now for the realistic conversation. People do not speak in complete
sentences in realistic dialogue. Men and women speak differently than
children. Old and young use different terms or slang. Different parts
of a country—such as the United States—may offer a wide scope of
language differences.

In this exchange from *Phantom in the Night,* the male protagonist
or hero is Nathan Drake and the female protagonist or heroine is Terri
Mitchell. Notice how the male speech pattern is shorter, more abrupt
sentences compared to the female's speech pattern.

Her [Terri] excitement deflated. "Are you a criminal?" No point in avoiding that question any longer.

"Depends on your definition of a criminal."

She shook her head. "That's not an encouraging reply."

"I don't want to encourage you."

That hurt, but she'd told him to be honest.

"You should pack up your grandmother and get out of here until this blows over," he said.

"My grandmother is away for a few days. I'll send her out to see her sister when she comes home. Much as I appreciate your concern, I can't turn my back on this case. There is a lot more at stake than just drug running, but that's all I'm willing to share."

He didn't move from where he leaned with arms crossed, but she could tell by how tight his fingers gripped his forearms he didn't care for her reticence to leave.

"In spite of what happened tonight," she continued, "I can take care of myself."

"Why don't you have a partner? Backup?"

"My business."

"Who do you work for?"

"Think I'll follow your lead and plead the fifth as well."

"Someone got that container yanked out from underneath the DEA and I doubt you have that kind of pull on your own."

She slapped the ice bag down on the placemat next to her arm. "You have no idea what kind of pull I have."

"I heard you left the DEA under questionable circumstances. If that's the case, I can't see how they'd fold under pressure from you."

He might not have meant to embarrass her, but he'd done a good job of it. "What I do and how I do it is none of your business."

"It is now."

Your characters are individuals. If they all sound alike then your story will sound as though it's full of drones. If they speak in complete sentences, your characters will sound like robots. You eat, sleep, talk, walk, and think your own way, differently than probably many people you know. Your characters need to be as different from one another as you are from family members, coworkers, friends, or strangers. Study family members, coworkers, friends, and strangers to pick up different personality traits and dialogue. Be careful not to create a character exactly like someone you know unless you plan to get a release. You can't just cover yourself by saying all the characters in this book are fictitious. Lawsuits have been won in spite of that disclaimer.

Dialogue must do more than just allow people to interact and chat. We want to eavesdrop on your characters. The dialogue will tell us as much about that character as what we learn in the story.

Use the questions in this template to assure your character's dialogue has significance, then give your story to someone else to read out loud. Someone unfamiliar with the story will not "anticipate" emotions and conversation. As you listen, words or phrases that don't flow will become more obvious. Also, you'll be free to make notes where you can tighten conversations.

DIALOGUE TEMPLATE

The purpose of this template is to push your dialogue to be as realistic as possible and to be used in a productive way.

Dialogue passage for this template is:

-----

1. What is the reason in the story that this conversation happened?

-----

2. Why is this conversation necessary to the story?

-----

3. Why did this conversation have to happen at this specific time in the story?

-----

4. What was each character feeling prior to this conversation?

-----

5. What has changed for each character after this conversation?

-----

6. Read the passage out loud. Does anything sound stilted? Do people around you talk this way? If not, rewrite the stilted parts and read it again.

    ----

7. Choose a line of dialogue for each person that would sound out of character for the other person to have spoken that way.

    ----

1. **What is the reason in the story that this conversation happened?**

    The reason this happens in the story, and at this
    point, is: a) the grandmother is in another city and
    currently considered "safe" (which becomes important
    very soon); b) Nathan knows about Terri having left
    the DEA under bad circumstances and he alludes to
    suspicions that she's connected to someone more
    powerful than the New Orleans Police Department to
    have gotten the container access; c) Terri admits
    this is more than a problem with drug dealers; d)
    motivation for Nathan to make a clear commitment to
    Terri and become involved with her problem if he's
    going to protect her.

2. **Why is this conversation necessary to the story?**

    To draw these two individuals into working together
    as a team because they now realize that they both
    have resources the other one can use to reach their
    individual objectives—Nathan to get revenge and Terri
    to stop a bad guy and redeem herself.

3. **Why did this conversation have to happen at this specific time in the
    story?**

    This leads up to Twist Point One (Chapter 8) where
    Terri and Nathan make an uneasy alliance that shifts
    the story line in a different direction.

4. **What was each character feeling prior to this conversation?**

    Terri was frustrated with her lack of clues and intel
    to bring down the bad guy, as well as to discover who
    the Phantom was and who he worked for. Nathan was
    focused on revenge, yet wary of getting Terri hurt in
    the crossfire if she was simply a good officer in the
    wrong place.

5. What has changed for each character after this conversation?

   With Nathan's help, Terri now stands a chance to take out the bad guy and prove her value to her new law enforcement agency. Helping Terri makes Nathan feel protective, which starts melting the emotional freeze he's experienced since he went to prison.

6. Read the passage out loud. Does anything sound stilted? Do people around you talk this way? If not, rewrite the stilted parts and read it again.

7. Choose a line of dialogue for each person that would sound out of character for the other person to have spoken that way.

   (Terri's internal and spoken dialogue would sound out of character if Nathan said it. Terri leads with her emotions and a lot of her conversation reveals how much she cares.) She wanted to drag him away from here, protect him from himself. "Do you have a death wish?"

   (Nathan and Terri speaking next where Nathan is much more direct and focused on reaching his goals, whether it's revenge or protecting her. Where a woman would try to negotiate the outcome, a man, particularly an alpha male, will simply make it clear he intends to reach the goal.)

   Terri—"Is that your bag over there?"

   Nathan—"I'm staying the night. I can bunk on the floor."

   Terri—"What if I say no?"

   Nathan—"I'll just break in after you go to sleep and still bunk on the floor."

Webster's Dictionary defines **final** as "Of or coming to an end; last. Deciding; concluding."

18 The Final Stage of Writing

> " I am definitely going to take a course on time management . . . just as soon as I can work it into my schedule. "
> —Louis E. Boone, author of *Contemporary Business*

At this point, you know your characters far better than before. Your plot has emotional depth, powerful action, twists and turns to keep your characters busy fighting their way to a big finish. Fast pacing is easier now that you have a way to test your scenes to ensure each one plays an integral part in linking the story together.

Now you're down to polishing the book. Find someone you trust to read your pages. This means someone who will give you honest feedback in a constructive manner. Friends and family are great supporters, but they aren't always the best place to test the story. Instead, find someone who reads the genre (mystery, fantasy, woman's fiction, science fiction, romance, young adult, etc.) of your story. Tell the reader to let you know if he or she was confused in places or "stopped reading" for any reason. If a reader shares this feedback, don't start explaining or justifying. Remember: You won't be able to travel with your manuscript to explain to an agent, editor or your future readers! If you can find more than one person to read your story then you'll know if those problems are consistent so you can revise the pages and fix something that may be the difference in an editor continuing to read or not.

Fresh Eyes

Read your story out loud to someone to catch mistakes and find any hiccups. It's even better if someone reads the story out loud to you, because he or she won't anticipate dialogue or action. Another piece of advice that is hard to follow, but valuable if you can be disciplined, is to let the completed book sit for at least thirty days untouched. You will be amazed at how many mistakes you'll catch before delivering your book to a reader or an editor. Some other home-stretch tips to keep in mind:

Watch out for new-writer mistakes such as including names that start with the same letter. It's confusing to keep a Martha, Mandy, and Martin straight in a story. Choose names that are as individual as the characters themselves.

Research thoroughly, but don't include everything you find on a topic in your story. Use the details surgically to convince the reader that the character knows his or her field of work or understands a particular piece of machinery. Don't load a scene with so much information it reads like a repair manual.

When describing someone or something, bring the details in close from the Point of View (POV) character. Show the action any time you can. Here's an example:
Basic description: Her trench coat and sneakers were soaked.
Active description: She held up a hand to stop him, the action almost regal and elegant in spite of her soaked trench coat and sneakers.

When in a character's POV, make sure that person "thinks" in a way that fits his or her gender, style, and dialogue, especially when in a female or male POV. Two examples follow:

POV of a young female who is an interior decorator and spots a piece of furniture in a store window: *What an exceptional example of a Louis XVI settee that would complete the Rothschild's summer villa.*

Middle-aged man who passes the same window: *Looks like that fancy couch Grandma had she used to yell at me to stay away from.*

 Remember that titles are subjective. Writers will tell you the title you choose for your story doesn't matter since the editor will change the title. That's not necessarily true. So choose your title well. Think about the genre you're targeting. If you are writing a taut suspense novel don't lean toward something too vague, literary, or fluffy-sounding. Think of your title as the first pitch of your book. Go to the library or local bookstore and peruse the books in the section where you see yours someday being shelved. Note what grabs your attention and try to mimic the hooks in those titles when you choose one for your book.

Finishing Your Story Is Half the Battle

There is only one guarantee in this business: If you don't finish the book and submit it, you are guaranteed not to sell. Most writers never finish a book and the reason is generally because they get "stuck." After working through these templates, you know how to finish your story. Once you've completed polishing your book, begin the submission process. (There are plenty of great reference books on the market that can walk you through how to submit a novel to an agent or editor.)

Give your story a chance to be read and be open to feedback. All really good books go through a revision process, so don't be disappointed if an editor or agent asks for revisions. If you receive suggestions on how to improve the story or weak areas of the story, ask if the editor would be interested in seeing the revised version. If the answer is yes, get busy! If the answer is no, still send a nice thank you and use those suggestions to improve your story for the next submission.

The Roman philosopher Seneca once said, "Luck is what happens when preparation meets opportunity." So make your luck and start a new book as soon as you finish the current one. The more you write the better a writer you will become and the better your chances are for selling your story.

Filmography

Alias (TV series) (2001–2006) Touchstone Television
Bad Boys (1995) Don Simpson/Jerry Bruckheimer Films
Bourne Identity (2002) Universal Pictures
Bridget Jones's Diary (2001) Little Bird Production Company
Casablanca (1942) Warner Pictures
A Christmas Carol (1938) Metro-Goldwyn-Mayer (MGM)
Chronicles of Riddick (2004) Universal Pictures
The Fifth Element (1997) Gaumont Production Company
Finding Nemo (2003) Walt Disney Pictures
Four Weddings and a Funeral (1994) Channel Four Films
Galaxy Quest (1999) DreamWorks SKG
G. I. Jane (1997) Caravan Pictures
Gladiator (2000) DreamWorks SKG
Gone with the Wind (1939) Selznick International Pictures
La Femme Nikita (TV series) (1997–2001) Baton Production Company
Lethal Weapon (1987) Silver Pictures
Lord of the Rings: The Fellowship of the Ring (2001) New Line Cinema
Men in Black (1997) Amblin Entertainment
Notting Hill (1999) Polygram Filmed Entertainment
Officer and a Gentleman (1982) Lorimar Film Entertainment
Overboard (1987) Hawn/Sylbert Movie Company
Pretty Woman (1990) Silver Screen Partners IV
Rain Man (1988) United Artists
Runaway Bride (1999) Interscope Communications
The Sixth Sense (1999) Barry Mendel Productions
Spider-Man (2002) Columbia Pictures Corporation
Star Wars (1977) Lucas Films
S. W. A. T. (2003) Columbia Pictures Corporation
Top Gun (1986) Paramount Pictures
The Wizard of Oz (1939) Metro-Goldwyn-Mayer (MGM)

Sources

Acevedo, Mario. Best-selling author of the Felix Gomez vampire-detective series from HarperCollins. (*www.marioacevedo.com*)

Austen, Jane. *Pride and Prejudice*, first published in 1813. Reprinted by Tark Classic Fiction, March, 2008.

Box, C. J. *New York Times* best-selling author of *Blue Heaven* (St. Martin's Minotaur) and *Blood Trail* (Putnam). (*www.cjbox.net*)

Brockmann, Suzanne. Excerpt (Pages 1–2) from *Out of Control* by *New York Times* best-selling author Suzanne Brockmann. Copyright © 2002 by Suzanne Brockman. Used by permission of Ballantine, an imprint of Random House, Inc. (*www.suzannebrockmann.com*)

Day, Alyssa. *New York Times* best-selling and RITA award-winning author of the Warriors of Poseidon series (Berkley Books). (*www.alyssaday.com*)

Franklin, Jon. Two-time Pulitzer Prize winner for nonfiction short stories published in the *Baltimore Evening Sun* (Baltimore, MD), and author of *Writing for Story* (Plume/Penguin).

Gaffney, Ed. Excerpts of pages 17, 24, and 25 are taken from *Suffering Fools* by legal thriller author Ed Gaffney. Copyright © 2006 by Edward G. Gaffney. Used by permission of Bantam Dell, an imprint of Random House, Inc. (*www.edgaffney.com*)

Haas, Roland. Best-selling author of *Enter the Past Tense: My Secret Life as a CIA Assassin* (Potomac Books, Inc.).

Hardegree, Maureen. Award-winning author whose stories are featured in the Mossy Creek Hometown series published by Belle Books. (*www.MaureenHardegree.com*)

Kenyon, Sherrilyn. *Dance with the Devil* (2003). St. Martin's Press. Sherrilyn is the #1 *New York Times* best-selling author of the famous Dark-Hunter series with over 12–15 million books in print. She also writes the Lords of Avalon series (Avon) as *New York Times* best-selling author Kinley MacGregor. (*www.SherrilynKenyon.com*)

Kenyon, Sherrilyn, and Dianna Love. *Phantom in the Night* (2008, Pocket Books).

Lawson, Margie. Author of *Deep Editing Power* lecture packets. (*www.MargieLawson.com*)

Mann, Catherine. Nationally known best-selling author of military-romance stories and a RITA award-winner with over a million books, which have sold in fifteen countries (Berkley). (*www.CatherineMann.com*)

Nunn, Mae. Award-winning author of the popular inspirational Texas Treasures series (Steeple Hill). (*www.MaeNunn.com*)

Parra, Kelly. RITA award finalist for her debut Young Adult book *Graffiti Girl* (MTV/Pocket). (*www.KellyParra.com*)

Pollero, Rhonda. *USA Today* best-selling and award-winning author of the Finley Anderson Tanner mysteries (*Kensington*). (*www.RhondaPollero.com*)

Rock, Joanne. Award-winning author of *A Knight Most Wicked* (Harlequin Historicals). (*www.JoanneRock.com*)

Smith, Haywood. *New York Times* best-selling and award-winning author of *The Red Hat Club* and *Wedding Belles* (St. Martin's Press). (*www.HaywoodSmith.net*)

White, Pat. Award-winning author of *Ring Around My Heart* (Dorchester). (*www.patwhitebooks.com*)

Wiggs, Susan. *New York Times* best-selling author of *Fireside*. (*www.susanwiggs.com*)

Index

About the Authors

Mary Buckham writes action-adventure novels, such as her award-winning *Invisible Recruit*. Prior to being published in book-length fiction, she was a magazine editor and contributing magazine editor. She has written hundreds of articles and has been published in book-length nonfiction. Currently she is a national writer's workshop presenter, both online and at live workshops around the United States and Canada. Mary is also hard at work on a thriller series. For more about Mary, visit *www.MaryBuckham.com*.

New York Times best-selling author Dianna Love started writing romantic suspense as she worked over a hundred feet in the air creating spectacular marketing projects for *Fortune* 500 companies. The first book she wrote (as Dianna Love Snell) sold, then the book went on to win the prestigious RITA award and her second one hit the *New York Times* bestseller list. She's currently cowriting a romantic-thriller series—the Bureau of American Defense stories—with #1 *New York Times* best-selling author Sherrilyn Kenyon. Their current release is *Whispered Lies* (Pocket/May 12, 2009). Dianna is a national speaker who teaches international workshops as well. For more on her fiction writing, visit *www.AuthorDiannaLove.com*.

To stay up to date on their highly successful writing programs and find out when their next Break Into Fiction® book will be released, visit *www.BreakIntoFiction.com*.